Promoting the Values
& Virtues of Classical
Education ✦

Classical Rhetoric

Logic & Rhetoric, Volume III

Thales Press   Raleigh, North Carolina

This book is the property of:

Thales Trivium:** **Logic & Rhetoric. Volumes I-III

Copyright 2023 by Thales Press.

First Edition. All rights reserved.

Thales Trivium:** **Logic & Rhetoric was published in Raleigh, North Carolina for use in
Thales Academy, a network of low-cost, high-quality private schools in North Carolina,
South Carolina, Tennessee, and Virginia.

All photos, unless otherwise noted, are available in the public domain.

Thales Press would like to thank and acknowledge the individuals who wrote the various
lessons in this textbook—namely, Winston Brady and Elizabeth Jetton. Josh Herring,
Director of the Thales debate program, wrote the chapters devoted to debate and public
speaking.

Special thanks to Andre Rusavek, Emma Mottor, Travis Copeland, Matt Ogle, Savannah
Blalock, and Alex Nolette for providing further edits and improvements to this work (and
others).

For more information and supplementary resources that include pacing guides, assess-
ments, project ideas, and other elements, email us at ***thalespress@thalesacademy.org***

Table of Contents

INDEPENDENCE HALL / PHILADELPHIA

Photo by Tyler Rutherford

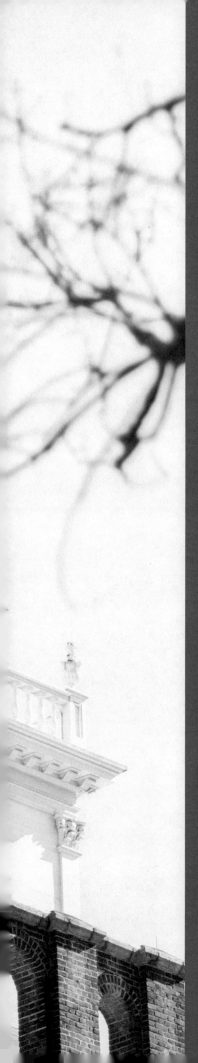

Section I
Classical Rhetoric

INDEPENDENCE HALL / PHILADELPHIA
Photo by Ernie Journeys

CHAPTER

The Five Canons of Rhetoric

ROADMAP

✦ Define the nature and purpose of classical rhetoric—what rhetoric is and for what purpose it should be used.

✦ Learn about the *Five Canons of Rhetoric.*

✦ Examine strategies and tips to help you become a better public speaker.

✦ Practice exercises to help you learn the material in this chapter.

THALES
OUTCOME

Nº 3

Unfailing integrity *exemplifies integrity while developing trusting relationships.*

The ancient world viewed rhetoric as the most important skill an individual could learn. The ancient world saw public speaking as an indispensable component of leadership and public service, and wealthy Greeks and Romans paid untold amounts of money to learn the art of rhetoric—but they did so to serve their own interests and advance their careers. In contrast, we learn rhetoric not to help ourselves alone but for the good of our neighbor. Leaders and orators should take every measure to use their gifts in a way that advances the common good.

What is Rhetoric?

SIMPLY ENOUGH, RHETORIC is the art of public speaking. That is, **rhetoric** is the skills and strategies one needs to put together a stirring speech, oftentimes with little to no preparation. The Greek philosopher **Aristotle** (384 - 322 BC) defined rhetoric as "the faculty of observing in any given case the available means of persuasion", whereas the Roman educator **Quintilian** defined oratory as "the art of speaking well" and that the "business of oratory [is] to think and speak rightly". Quintilian argues that rhetoric and public speaking are indeed the highest of arts for any well-educated person. He states that it is by oratory that a virtuous individual could "defend his friends, direct a senate or people by his counsels, or lead an army to whatever enterprise he may desire". Oratory, subsequently, is not just the ability to speak or to plead, "but as was the case with Pericles," the ability "to hurl forth lightning and thunder" (Quintilian 104).

At times, the word *rhetoric* may be used synonymously with *oratory* or *public speaking*. Rhetoric was the capstone of an education in the ancient and medieval world. As we discussed in chapter 1, students from 8 to 14 years of age would progress through the **trivium**, the "three ways" that culminate in an individual of learning and distinction, the three ways being grammar, logic, and rhetoric. Grammar encompassed the fundamental rules of Latin grammar and the rules by which an individual could write clearly; logic encompassed the rules of argumentation so that an individual could reason effectively; lastly, rhetoric marshaled the rules of grammar and logic to speak effectively. The orator could bring his or her words, thoughts, and arguments together to deliver a speech that fit whatever the occasion called for. Rhetoric encompassed all the skills needed to argue rightly on a subject and compose a speech that is logically sound, aesthetically pleasing, and powerfully delivered so that the audience is inspired to take up the course of action expounded upon by the orator.

As such, two important considerations should be kept in mind. First, that rhetoric is a counterpart to **logic**. In a speech, the rules of logical argumentation are arranged in such a way as to sound pleasing and persuasive when they are delivered before an audience. The skills we have learned in logic and have practiced in debate are now formally incorporated into rhetoric for the purposes of composing sound, reasoned, and effective speeches. Moreover, as logic aims for truth, we should practice rhetoric in a spirit of truth, personal integrity, and

Rhetoric is the art of public speaking, which, in the ancient world, was seen as the most important skill a leader could have. The goal of rhetoric is to know what is good and to persuade others to choose what is good, too.

Vocabulary

Write down this vocabulary your notebook. These terms will help you better learn and understand this material.

Rhetoric

The art of public speaking, which the ancient world considered an important component of public service. The word *rhetoric* may be used synonymously with *oratory* and *public speaking*.

Aristotle

A Greek philosopher who lived from 384 to 322 BC; his writings on *Politics, Poetics, Physics, Metaphysics,* and *Rhetoric* form the basis for much of the Western canon.

Quintilian

A Roman educator who lived from 35 to 100 AD; he believed that the ideal orator should not only be an eloquent speaker but also a lover of wisdom and virtue.

Trivium

A three-fold approach to education that began with grammar, continued with logic, and ended with rhetoric; the metaphorical place where the "three roads" of grammar, logic, and rhetoric met.

Logic

The art of right thinking and the ability to make sense of a wide array of facts and organize them into a coherent system.

QUINTILIAN / AD 35 - 100

Roman educator and author of On the Institutes of Oratory

self-control. We should never use the powers of persuasion to serve ourselves or to dress up falsehoods like truths. Instead, we should use the skills we will learn in rhetoric to help others know what is good and choose what is best.

Second, that public speaking and rhetoric are indispensable skills for leaders, a truth that is as important in the modern world as it was in the ancient world. A good leader must know how to arrange and deliver a speech in order to move the hearts of men to a particular course of action. This moving power of rhetoric was as true for the ancient world and figures like Demosthenes, Pericles, and Cicero, and it is true for the modern world and seminal leaders such as Abraham Lincoln, Frederick Douglass, and Martin Luther King, Jr. The ideal orator, then, must not only be a good public speaker, but he or she must also be committed to the cultivation of truth and the pursuit of what is good, what is true, and what is beautiful. They should recognize the right and true course of action, a cause greater than the speaker's immediate self-interest, and inspire their audience to take up that task "whatever the cost may be", to quote Winston Churchill. The ancient world equated public service with public speaking, and the most noteworthy leaders were often marked for their eloquence and their public speaking skills.

Noteworthy Orators, Ancient and Modern

|| DEMOSTHENES / 384 - 322 BC

|| SIR WINSTON CHURCHILL / 1874 - 1965

|| CICERO / 106 - 43 BC

|| DR. MARTIN LUTHER KING JR. / 1929 - 1964

How is logic the counterpart of rhetoric?

How should an orator use his or her gifts of public speaking?

The Five Canons of Rhetoric

IF YOU'VE EVER GIVEN A SPEECH, you know how difficult it is to think of a topic and compose an address. In the ancient world, ambitious Greeks and Romans would seek out famed teachers of rhetoric and oratory to teach them how to complete this process. Teachers of rhetoric could command large sums of money by teaching wealthy students how to compose and deliver speeches, particularly when they did not have much time to prepare a speech. To simplify the process, Roman rhetoricians taught their students to plan their speeches using a method called the **Five Canons of Rhetoric**. The word **canon** comes from a Greek word for a type of reed used as a measuring rod; thus, the word *canon* refers to a set of standards or criteria by which we judge something like a book, a movie, or a speech. The Five Canons of Rhetoric are as follows: *inventio, dispositio, elocutio, memoria,* and *pronuntiatio.*

Inventio: The discovery, or the *invention*, of the idea, as well as the most effective means of arguing for that idea.

Dispositio: The arrangement of the material in your speech, paper, or other mode of communication.

Elocutio: The style of presentation, such as the rhetorical and literary devices you put into your paper.

Memoria: The process of memorizing your speech.

Pronuntiatio: The process of delivering your speech.

The Roman educator Quintilian held up Cicero as the figure closest to his *ideal orator*—that is, Cicero was not only eloquent and persuasive but also an individual of great integrity and virtue. Cicero lived from 106 to 43 BC in the twilight years of the Roman Republic. As a lawyer and a Roman senator, Cicero had to give speeches almost every day of his career, often without any prior preparation. He was also a philosopher who wrote a series of Plato-like dialogues on various topics related to philosophy, including ones devoted to rhetoric. In *On the Character of an Orator*, Cicero wrote about the art of writing and delivering a speech:

> *Since all the business and art of an orator is divided into five parts [the five canons], he ought first to find out what he should say; next, to dispose and arrange his matter, not only in a certain order, but with a sort of power and judgment; then to clothe and deck his thoughts with language; then to secure them in his memory; and lastly, to deliver them with dignity and grace (40-41).*

Let us can unpack Cicero's words here and examine the five canons of rhetoric in greater detail.

Inventio: *Find out what we should say*

The **inventio** is the *invention* or *discovery* of a topic and the best means of arguing for your position. Everything else follows from that idea. For example, the arrangement of your material (the **dispositio**) flows from your idea (the *inventio*), for the *dispositio* is the systematic and orderly arrangement of your material in support of your argument (we will cover the *dispo-*

Vocabulary

*Write down this vocabulary
in your notebook or use
the special Guided Notes
worksheet provided at the end
of this chapter.*

Five Canons of Rhetoric
The five most important
components of a speech.

Canon
The word *canon* comes from
the Greek for *measuring rod*
and refers to the standard or
the criteria by which a piece of
human culture is judged.

Inventio
Not only the discovery, or
invention, of the idea, but also
the most effective means of
arguing for that idea.

Dispositio
The arrangement or the
outline of the material in your
speech, paper, or other mode of
communication.

Declamation
Rhetorical exercises for
students to practice composing
and delivering speeches.

Elocutio
The canon of style; the way in
which you express your points
in a manner appropriate for the
occasion.

Memoria
The process of memorizing
your speech.

Pronuntiatio
The process of delivering your
speech.

CICERO / THE CATALINE ORATIONS
Cicero denounces Cataline on the floor of the Senate.

sitio in chapter 26, entitled *The Six Parts of Discourse*). The *inventio* answers the question, "What should I say?" while the dispositio answers the question, "How do I arrange what I say, once I know what to say?"

To help their students develop the ability to devise speeches with little preparation time, ancient teachers of rhetoric gave their students special exercises called **declamations**. These exercises were essentially prompts that outlined some common problem, some drawn from legal cases, some from ancient history, and others from every day life. Students then devised what they thought the best means of arguing for that position and adapted their speech accordingly. These were opportunities to practice, for if one does not know how to argue, or does not feel confident arguing, the best thing to do is keep trying. We have provided some sample *declamation* exercises at the end of this chapter.

Dispositio: Dispose and arrange his matter, not only in a certain order, but with a sort of power and judgment

The *dispositio* is the arrangement of the material in a speech, a process referred to as the *Six Parts of Discourse*. The Six Parts of Discourse include the introduction to a speech (the *exordium*), the speaker's explanation of the case under discussion (the *narratio*), an outline of the speaker's main points (the *divisio*), the proof or evidence in support of the speaker's points (the *confirmatio*), a list of, and answers to, the opposing arguments (the *confutatio*), and the conclusion of the speech (the *peroratio*). We will cover the Six Parts of Discourse in later chapters.

Elocutio: To clothe and deck his thoughts with language

Elocutio, meanwhile, deals with style and word choice in either a speech or a written composition. Simply enough, elocution is the ability to speak clearly, but in the ancient world, elocution had everything to do with style: how you say something and why you say it the way you do. You must tailor the style in which you express your points with the occasion, your audience, and the purpose of your speech.

Memoria: To secure them in his memory

The canon of **memoria** is the memorization of a speech. Memorizing speeches is key to delivering them with great effect and intensity. But of course, memorizing a speech of any considerable length is difficult, and it takes time to develop the skill of memorization, for memorization is a skill like any other. Quintilian recommends that students practice when they are still young, learning "portions of speeches by heart and deliver[ing] them standing, with a loud voice, and exactly as he will have to plead so that he may consequently exercise by pronunciation both his voice and his memory" (*On the Education of an Orator*). The earlier students discipline themselves to memorize material of any considerable length, the easier and more natural it will become to memorize information in general.

Pronuntiatio: Lastly, to deliver them with dignity and grace

The **pronuntiatio**, the last of the five canons of rhetoric, is the delivery of one's speech. That is, how loudly, clearly, and eloquently one can deliver a speech before an assembled crowd. The human voice is like a musical instrument, and, as such, orators should do everything they can to take care of that instrument. Orators may want to avoid drinking milk or cold water before a speech since these liquids may negatively affect their vocal cords. Aspiring orators could also learn from the Athenian statesman Demosthenes who, according to legend, practiced his speeches while running, with rocks in his mouth, and in front of the crashing waves at the beach. That way, he could work on his lung capacity, elocution, and his ability to project his voice as loudly and clearly as possible.

BIG IDEA

The Five Canons of Rhetoric *constituted the most important elements that went into composing and delivering a speech, from thinking of the best way to argue for a position to giving the speech in the most effective way possible.*

Guided Notes / The Five Canons of Rhetoric

Instructions: Given the amount of vocabulary in this chapter, take a moment to write down a definition for each term in the table provided below.

Vocabulary Word	Definition
Rhetoric	
Five Canons of Rhetoric	
Inventio	
Dispositio	
Elocutio	
Memoria	
Pronuntiatio	

The Inventio and Declamations

Instructions: In ancient Rome and Greece, teachers of rhetoric would give their students topics to practice their ability to compose speeches with relatively-little preparation time. These exercises were called *declamations*; in the space provided, write out the best means of arguing on that particular topic. In light of the unique nature of this exercise, you could write out the introduction to a speech you could give—a short paragraph with one or two reasons why your position provides the best course of action; you could write a paragraph explaining what would be the best course of action and how you might argue for one position or another; or you could weigh all the possible arguments *for* and *against* one position or another. Your answer, in part, depends on the *inventio*, the best means of arguing for a position that you, the aspiring-orator, decide. All in all, answer each question in a paragraph of 100 to 150 words.

You and the other members of the student council are deciding on what to do for an upcoming service project. You believe that the best service project would be a visit to a local nursing home to spend time with the residents, playing games and hearing stories. How might you convince your peers to go to this nursing home?

The Inventio and Declamations

Instructions: In light of the unique nature of this exercise, you could write out the introduction to a speech you could give—a short paragraph with one or two reasons why your position provides the best course of action; you could write a paragraph explaining what would be the best course of action and how you might argue for one position or another; or you could weigh all the possible arguments *for* and *against* one position or another. Your answer, in part, depends on the *inventio*, the best means of arguing for a position that you, the aspiring-orator, decide. All in all, answer each question in a paragraph of 100 to 150 words.

> You are a student in class, and the teacher leaves the room. One student suggests that they lock the door as a means of disrupting class. How might you discourage that student from taking this action?

The Inventio and Declamations

Instructions: In light of the unique nature of this exercise, you could write out the introduction to a speech you could give—a short paragraph with one or two reasons why your position provides the best course of action; you could write a paragraph explaining what would be the best course of action and how you might argue for one position or another; or you could weigh all the possible arguments *for* and *against* one position or another. Your answer, in part, depends on the *inventio*, the best means of arguing for a position that you, the aspiring-orator, decide. All in all, answer each question in a paragraph of 100 to 150 words.

You are Fabius, the general in charge of the Roman legions during the Second Punic War. Your generals disagree with your decision to avoid fighting Hannibal in the field. How might you persuade them that your decision is the best course of action?

The Inventio and Declamations

Instructions: In light of the unique nature of this exercise, you could write out the introduction to a speech you could give—a short paragraph with one or two reasons why your position provides the best course of action; you could write a paragraph explaining what would be the best course of action and how you might argue for one position or another; or you could weigh all the possible arguments *for* and *against* one position or another. Your answer, in part, depends on the *inventio*, the best means of arguing for a position that you, the aspiring-orator, decide. All in all, answer each question in a paragraph of 100 to 150 words.

You are Patrick Henry, and the year is 1775. You must convince the members of the Second Virginia Convention to embrace the cause of independence as their own even as the military might of the British Empire is bearing down upon the American colonies. How would you inspire your colleagues to take up a cause that could lead to their ruin and death?

CHAPTER

The Canon of Style

ROADMAP

✦ Define *elocutio*, the canon of style.

✦ Discover the difference between a high, moderate, and low style.

✦ Learn rhetorical devices that may, if used correctly, add style to your speeches.

THALES
OUTCOME

Nº 13

A person with **Well-Developed People and Communication Skills** *executes effective interpersonal and communication skills, taking into account the audience and positive outcomes.*

Elocutio, the canon of *style*, focuses on tailoring the content of your speech in a way best suited to occasion. Style also includes a special kind of figurative language called *rhetorical devices* which can make your speech more effective and memorable.

The Canon of Style

THE THIRD OF THE FIVE canons of rhetoric is the *elocutio*. Simply put, **elocutio** is style—the way in which you express your points in a manner appropriate for the occasion. *Elocutio*, or our modern English word *elocution*, focuses on style and word choice in either a speech or a written composition. Elocution is the ability to speak clearly, but in the ancient world, elocution had everything to do with style: how you say something and why you say it the way you do. The first rule of elocution, however, is clarity: no matter how you say something, it must be clear enough for people to understand it. In *On the Orator*, Cicero writes:

> *What manner of elocution can be better (for I will consider action by-and-by) than that of speaking in pure Latin, with clarity of speech, with gracefulness, and with aptitude and congruity to the subject in question? Of the two which I mentioned first, purity and clearness of language, I do not suppose that any account is expected from me; for we do not attempt to teach him to be an orator who can not speak (202).*

But what kind of style is appropriate to the occasion? Orators must adapt their style and the way in which they express their points to the occasion, the audience, and the purpose of the speech. As a result, teachers of rhetoric differentiated between the kinds of style. The three different kinds of style are as follows:

Attentuata: A low or plain style, most appropriate for instructing.

Mediocre *or* **Robusta:** A middle or forcible style, most appropriate for moving or exhorting one's audience.

Gravis *or* **Florid**: A style that may be serious (*gravis*) or beautiful (*florid*) and which uses a rare and highly-elevated word choice, rhetorical devices, and a highly-developed, beautiful-sounding sentence structure. Such a style is most appropriate for a eulogy at a funeral or a graduation speech and other similar, solemn occasions. Quintilian says that this style is most appropriate for persuading or even *charming* an audience. While it is similar in principle to the middle style of speaking in a *mediocre* or *robusta* fashion, such a style differs by degree. For example, the speaker may use more rhetorical devices or a more elevated diction.

Style focuses heavily on word choice and the words that are most appropriate for the occasion. If you are instructing a group of students, you want to use words that are simple and clear. If moving or exhorting, use words that express urgency and importance; in charming, words that are flowery and rich. Consider writing with a thesaurus close by, so as to go with words that are not only more inventive and lively, but also fit the context of your writing better.

Regardless of the style you feel best fits your purpose and your audience, you should strive to write with clear subjects and strong, active verbs. Do not rely too heavily on the verb *to be* in your writing, but try to systematically replace words like *is, was, were,* or *are*

Vocabulary

Write down this vocabulary in your notebook. These terms will help you better learn and understand the material in this chapter.

Elocutio
The canon of style; the way in which you express your points in a manner appropriate for the occasion.

Attentuata
A low or plain style, most appropriate for instructing.

Mediocre or Robusta
A middle or forcible style, most appropriate for moving or exhorting one's audience.

Gravis or Florid
A heavy or florid style, most appropriate for charming.

Rhetorical Device
An arrangement of words in such a way that these words sound more pleasing, carry more meaning, and thus should be more memorable.

Chiasmus
The careful balancing of clauses in a sentence, so that words and concepts are repeated and the same grammatical structure is used, but the words are arranged in a different order from one clause to the next.

Polysyndeton
The excessive use of conjunctions in a sentence in order to convey a sense of excitement and urgency.

with precise, active verbs. Consider a sentence like *Latin is exciting* as opposed to *Latin excites* or *Latin spurs* or *Latin inspires*, or any other strong active verb with which you can replace the word *is*. Many good writers use this strategy to find and use better words in their stories, speeches, and papers—and you should use this strategy, too!

Rhetorical Devices

Think of famous speeches you have heard or even short phrases that have since become some of the most famous phrases in American history. What made those speeches effective? What made their words not only pleasing and delightful but also easy to remember?

In short, these speeches were effective and memorable because the writers took time to arrange their words and sentences for maximum effect and integrate rhetorical devices into their speeches. A **rhetorical device** is an arrangement of words in such a way that these words sound more pleasing, carry more meaning, and thus should be more memorable. It was not enough to simply have words to say. The one who could convey his message in the most beautiful arrangement won the day in classical rhetoric.

Below are several rhetorical devices used by some of the most famous leaders in world history (and one from Dr. Seuss).

Chiasmus: Perhaps the most famous and often-used rhetorical device is *chiasmus*, taken from the Greek letter *x*. Chiasmus is the careful balancing of clauses in a sentence, so that words and concepts are repeated and the same grammatical structure is used, but the words are arranged in a different order from one clause to the next.

Example: *Ask not what your country can do for you--ask what you can do for your country*, from John F. Kennedy's Inaugural Address.

Polysyndeton: The excessive use of conjunctions in a sentence in order to convey a sense of excitement and urgency.

Example from Dr. Seuss' *Yertle the Turtle*:

You stay in your place while I sit here and rule.

I'm king of a cow! And I'm king of a mule!

I'm king of a house! And a bush! And a cat!

But that isn't all. I'll do better than that!

The repetitive use of the conjunction *and* emphasizes the megalomaniac desires of King Yertle, a turtle who equates the glory of his reign with the number of turtles that comprise his throne.

Parallelism: The use of grammatically-balanced words, phrases, or clauses in a speech, which not only sound better but also convey a sense of balance and order.

Example from Abraham Lincoln's *Gettysburg Address*, delivered in 1863:

It is rather for us to be here dedicated to the great task remaining before us—that from these honored dead we take increased devotion to that cause for which they here gave the last full measure of devotion—that we here highly resolve that these dead shall not have died in vain—that this nation, under God, shall have a new birth of freedom, and that government of the people, by the people, for the people, shall not perish from the earth.

In the last clause, Lincoln repeats the phrase *the people* to remind his listeners that the Civil War, the sacrifices of civilians and soldiers alike, and the grand experiment in self-government that is the United States of America are all inextricably linked together.

Anaphora: The repetition of key words or phrases from one sentence to another in order to reinforce the author's purpose.

Here is an example from Winston Churchill's speech to the House of Commons in June, 1940:

We shall fight on the beaches, we shall fight on the landing grounds, we shall fight in the fields and in the streets, we shall fight in the hills; we shall never surrender.

Notice the repeated phrase *we shall fight* that reinforces Churchill's purpose and resolve in resisting Nazi tyranny.

Alliteration: The repetition of key consonant sounds in a sentence or clause.

Here is an example from John Milton's description of Satan in *Paradise Lost*:

At first, as one who sought access, but fear'd

To interrupt, side-long he works his way.

As when a Ship by skilful Stearsman wrought

Nigh Rivers mouth or Foreland, where the Wind

Veres oft, as oft so steers, and shifts her Saile

In the poem, Milton emphasizes Satan's transformation into a snake with *hiss*-like *s* sounds, the kind of hissing sound a snake would make (*Paradise Lost*, 9. 511-515).

Zeugma: A verb or an adjective that is used in two different ways and thus joins together two different parts of a sentence. Here is an example from Mark Twain's *The Adventures of Tom Sawyer*:

They tugged and tore at each other's hair and clothes, punched and scratched each other's nose, and covered themselves with dust and glory.

The tussling character in Twain's classic novel covered themselves in literal dust but only metaphorical glory, but the two images juxtaposed together makes the scene especially entertaining.

Vocabulary

Parallelism
The use of grammatically-balanced words, phrases, or clauses in a speech which not only sound better but also convey a sense of balance and order.

Anaphora
The repetition of key words or phrases from one sentence to another in order to reinforce the author's purpose.

Alliteration
The repetition of a key consonant sound in a sentence or a speech.

Zeugma
A verb or an adjective that is used in two different ways and thus joins together two different parts of a sentence.

Noteworthy Orators and Poets, Ancient and Modern

|| JOHN F. KENNEDY / 1917 - 1963

|| JOHN MILTON / 1608 - 1674

|| WINSTON CHURCHILL / 1874 - 1965

|| ABRAHAM LINCOLN / 1809 - 1865

For your next paper, speech, or any other assignment of significance, try and compose one meaningful rhetorical device and put it into your work. Try to use a rhetorical device that serves the purposes of your speech—if you have a meaningful, beautiful point you hope your audience will remember, phrase that point in the form of a chiasmus; if you have a series of meaningful points, use anaphora; and so on. Remember, the words of your speech are your means of moving the audience to that idea or position you believe is in their best interest, so make those words count!

What style is most appropriate for teaching? What style is most appropriate for exhorting? For charming?

Should an orator put rhetorical devices into even the simplest of styles? Why or why not?

Style and Occasion

Instructions: Below are three possible scenarios where you as the speaker must persuade someone of the best course of action. What style—*attentuata*, *mediocre* or *robusta*, *gravis* or *florid*—is most appropriate for each occasion? Explain your reasoning in one or two sentences.

If you were a teacher trying to explain a math problem to a student, what style would you use and why? Explain your reasoning.

If you were a coach trying to encourage your team to keep playing hard against your much better opponents, what style would you use and why? Explain your reasoning.

If you were giving the speech at a graduation ceremony, what style would you use and why? Explain your reasoning.

03
CHAPTER

On Memory

ROADMAP

✦ Define *memoria*, the canon of *memory*.

✦ Examine the importance of memorizing your speech or, at least, preparing your speech so that it seems as if you did memorize it.

✦ Learn skills and strategies to make the process of memorizing easier and more efficient for you.

THALES OUTCOME

№ 8

A person with **Astute Problem Solving** *plans the best possible solutions to challenges to achieve optimal success.*

The canon of *memoria*, that of *memory*, may be the easiest canon to learn but is by far the hardest to master. In this chapter, we will provide tips to make the difficult task of memorizing speeches easier and more efficient for you, as well as strategies to deliver a speech as if you memorized it, even if you didn't have the time needed to do so.

On Memory

THE LAST TWO CANONS, **memoria** and **pronuntiatio** focus on the memorization and the delivery, respectively, of your speech. We shall begin with the canon of *memoria*, because memorizing a speech will also help you to deliver that speech with greater effect. Of course, memorizing a speech of any considerable length is difficult. To memorize even a short speech might take hours of difficult mental and even physical work if you write down the speech multiple times. Yet, memorization is a skill like any other. Quintilian recommends that students practice when they are still young, learning "portions of speeches by heart and deliver[ing] them standing, with a loud voice, and exactly as he will have to plead so that he may consequently exercise by pronunciation both his voice and his memory". The earlier that students devote themselves to memorizing material of any considerable length, the easier and more natural it will become to memorize more and more information.

As a result, you should practice memorizing shorter compositions to prepare the way for memorizing longer works. You can choose shorter poems, maxims, excerpts from plays, or meaningful song lyrics and commit those to memory. Memorizing these pieces will condition your mind to take in, absorb, and retain more information than if you never undertook the intellectual labor involved in memorization. If you select notable speeches, then you will have the added benefit of internalizing the rhythms, the cadences, the word choice, style, and syntax of these great orators and imbibe lessons from them you may not have gotten simply by reading their work. Quintilian adds that students gain more experience and oratorical skill by memorizing the speeches of skilled orators than if they memorized their own speeches.

To aid in memorization, start small. First, select a passage of an appropriate length—long enough for you to feel accomplished in memorizing it, short enough that you will be successful. Start at the beginning and read the first clause out loud, then repeat it over and over again, perhaps upwards of five to ten times. Then, see if you can recite that clause without looking at it. Add on the next clause, and repeat the same process until you finish the first sentence you wish to memorize. Then, see if can you repeat the whole sentence from the beginning without making any mistakes. If not, continue reading it over and saying it out loud until its words are committed to memory. Continue this process for each subsequent sentence until you have successfully memorized the entire passage.

A second method is to build a *house of memory*. That is, you create a conceptual, mental framework for your speech (and its points) in your mind; then, as you deliver the speech, you walk through the "rooms" (the points) of that speech. Each point or section of your speech is a different "room," and as you walk through the house and explore each room, you remember (and thus deliver) the parts of that speech. This method is particularly effective for visual learners.

Memorization is a skill not unlike the skills in any sport; you will have to practice if you want to improve. Identify times in the day when you can recite the passage in whole or in part so that you do not forget it and thus lose the hard work you have devoted to memorizing it. In this process, it is important not to feel frustrated. Memorization may be hard at first, but if you give yourself enough time, you will be amazed at what you can accomplish and commit to memory. In addition, memorization sharpens the mind and the intellect in a way few other academic skills can. The process should not only become easier, but you may also improve in your other subjects as well. To aid in memorizing your speech, practice, practice, practice your material over and over again. Consider reading your speech or your presentation over many times, especially as you write it. Or refrain from writing the speech down to begin with. Instead, compose the speech orally—that is, out loud—while you are doing other things such as gardening, exercising, or driving.

If you find that you just can't memorize a speech in the time you have, there are other solutions to help you deliver your speech. These solutions can even give the appearance that you memorized it. First, work from a series of speaking aids like note cards or an outline. If you know your speech well enough, you can use your outline to help you stay on track, especially if you find you have forgotten any of the key transition points. Include statistical data you know you can't remember during a speech. If you know you stumble at a particular part in your speech, make a special note of it on your outline or on your note cards, and practice that part in particular. Don't let it take you by surprise.

Even if you intend to read from a prepared manuscript, you should still practice reading your speech multiple times. That way, your delivery sounds more natural and free-flowing. In addition, the transitions, those moments when you shift from one section to

WINSTON CHURCHILL / 1874 - 1965
Prime Minster of Great Britain

another, are generally the hardest to remember and deliver, so even if you have memorized the speech, you may want to keep an outline in front of you. Winston Churchill (above) is perhaps one of the greatest orators in modern history. He memorized some speeches and employed a fairly novel technique for others. When Churchill addressed the House of Commons, he would write his prepared speech in large print with gaps in between his sentences. When Churchill finished one sentence, he would take a meaningful pause, look down at his prepared notes, identify what he was to say next, and then continue speaking. You can employ the same technique with note cards that include key statistics and figures you may have trouble memorizing.

The Canon of Memoria / Exercises

Of the five canons, the canon of *memoria* may be the hardest canon to master. The practice of memorizing a speech requires considerable time and effort, but, like any skill, memorizing a speech becomes easier and easier the more things you try to memorize. In later chapters, we will provide short selections from various speeches your teacher may ask you to memorize.

For now, let us hone our ability to memorize by trying to commit to memory a series of maxims and aphorisms from Benjamin Franklin. Most of these maxims come from *Poor Richard's Almanack,* written and published by Franklin in the years 1732 to 1758. These maxims are short and pithy and contain some kind of parallel grammatical structure (i.e., the clauses in each maxim employ the same kind of words and in the same order), which makes them easier to memorize. Notice, too, Franklin's use of zeugma, in that Franklin uses one verb or adjective in two different ways. Given the difficulty of memorizing anything, identify one or two of these maxims as worthy of committing to memory and start from there.

Quotations from *Poor Richard* taken from the Franklin Institute, <u>accessible here</u>.

1. *Look before, or you'll find yourself behind*, 1735.

2. *Well done is better than well said.*

3. *What you seem to be, be really*, 1744.

4. *No gains without pains*, 1745.

5. *He that lies down with Dogs, shall rise up with fleas*, 1733.

6. *Better slip with foot than tongue*, 1734.

7. *Glass, China, and Reputation, are easily crack'd, and never well mended*, 1750.

8. *Wish not so much to live long as to live well*, 1738.

9. *Lost Time is never found again*, 1747.

10. *A true Friend is the best Possession*, 1744.

11. *Haste makes Waste*, 1753.

12. *It is better to take many Injuries than to give one*, 1735.

The Canon of Memoria / Exercises

The canon of *memoria* may be the hardest to master, but it is possible to memorize speeches through practice over a long period of time. One way to memorize is to recite a small portion of the speech, one line or sentence at a time until you have committed that part to memory. Then, move on to the next sentence, repeating it out loud or perhaps writing it down on paper until you have memorized that part, too. Then, return to the beginning of the speech and recite the two sentences you have memorized, and repeat this process until you have memorized the speech in its entirety, but be careful to give yourself enough time. Such an exercise needs days of continued practice and cannot be started the night before you have to deliver a speech or recite a memorized poem or speech as part of an assignment.

In the following chapters, we will begin analyzing noteworthy speeches from American history from such famous orators as Patrick Henry, Frederick Douglass, and Abraham Lincoln, Each chapter will close with an opportunity to commit to memory one passage from that speech according to this method. Your teacher may or may not ask you to complete the assignment, but the process of memorization is so valuable we hope that you will practice these steps whenever you encounter a poem or a passage you wish never to forget. These exercises will follow the speeches included in the following chapters.

Example / Step and Description	Example
Step 1: Read the first clause or sentence out loud upwards of five to ten times. Try to recite the sentence without looking at the words.	*You would be amazed at what you can accomplish …*
Step 2: Read the next clause or sentence out loud upwards of five to ten times. Try to recite the sentence without looking at the words.	*If you devoted a few minutes each day to a task that, at the beginning, seemed impossible …*
Step 3: Go back to the beginning and repeat the first two clauses or sentences. Repeat until you have memorized the passage in question.	*You would be amazed at what you can accomplish if you devoted a few minutes each day to a task that, at the beginning, seemed impossible…*
Suggested Assignment: Recite the speech from memory for a homework, classwork, or assessment grade with one point for each word memorized (may also be taken as a percentage).	———

CHAPTER

The Delivery

ROADMAP

✦ Learn about the *pronuntiatio*, the *delivery* of your speech .

✦ Understand why the *delivery* of your speech may be the most important of the five canons.

✦ Discover practical tips to help you deliver your speech.

THALES
OUTCOME

№ 7

A person with **Competent Technical Skills** *applies technical skills to manage personal and educational outcomes.*

A speech is a unique form of communication in that a speech can only be given once. Even if a speaker gives a speech multiple times, the speaker must deliver that speech effectively in the moment of delivery. As a result, the *pronuntiatio,* or the *delivery*, of your speech is one of the most important parts of the rhetorical process. Thankfully, we can practice our ability to deliver a speech for maximum effectiveness through the strategies we will present in this chapter.

The Delivery

THE FIFTH CANON OF RHETORIC is the **pronuntiatio,** the delivery of your speech. Like *memoria*, the *pronuntiatio*, or the *delivery*, may be easy to learn but hard to master. Pronuntiatio focuses on the delivery of your speech and how effective you are in physically communicating the content of your speech. While it may be desirable to write your speech ahead of time, and your listeners may be interested in reading a copy of your speech afterwards, it remains that a speech is a unique work of art in that it can only be delivered once—and that before an audience of people. The delivery of a speech is like an arrow flying towards its target, and the canon of *pronuntiatio* is designed to help our words fly as straight and smooth as possible. One can pour the very best arguments and rhetorical devices into a speech, but if the voice of the orator cannot be heard, then all of that hard work and preparation is for nothing.

While it is obvious that students can improve in public speaking by signing up for more opportunities to speak in public, there are other ways that students can prepare for a speech so as to deliver it for maximum effectiveness. Consider, for instance, the example of the Athenian orator Demosthenes. Demosthenes lived in Athens from 384 to 322 BC, and he is famous for delivering a series of speeches against the looming threat of Macedon, whose king, Philip II, had grand ambitions to conquer all of Greece. Demosthenes recognized the unique threat that Macedon posed to the free and independent city-states of Greece, and he used all of his oratorical abilities to persuade his fellow Athenians to resist Macedon and retain their independence.

And yet, according to legend, Demosthenes was laughed out of the Athenian assembly at the first speech he gave. Cicero wrote the following description of Demosthenes and the challenges Demosthenes overcame in *On Oratory*:

> *Demosthenes excelled all other orators in ardor and perseverance, for he overcame, first of all, the impediments of nature by pains and diligence; and though his voice was so inarticulate that he was unable to pronounce the first letter of the very art which he was so eager to acquire, he accomplished so much by practice that no one is thought to have spoken more distinctly; and though his breath was short, he effected such improvement by holding it in while he spoke, that in one sequence of words (as his writings show) two risings and two fallings of his voice were included; and he also (as is related) after putting pebbles into his mouth, used to pronounce several verses at the highest pitch of his voice without taking a breath, not standing in one place, but walking forward, and mounting a steep ascent. With such encouragements as these... youths should be incited to study and industry.*

According to legend, in order to improve his delivery, Demosthenes practiced his speeches while running to improve his stamina and breath control. He delivered his speeches with rocks in his mouth to hone his ability to articulate difficult words, and he even recited his speeches in front of the roaring ocean to improve his ability to project his voice. All of these things helped Demosthenes to become a better public speaker, perhaps more so than if he did not have any challenges to overcome. That should give all of us the confidence to become better public speakers and leaders by taking small steps toward self-improvement. We will cover many of those small steps in this chapter.

|| DEMOSTHENES / 384 - 322 BC

The *pronuntiatio* is more physical and tangible than the other canons. When delivering a speech, students have to focus on the volume of their voice, tone, mannerisms, even their hand gestures. In short, we have to be mindful of an entire network of interdependent actions that occur while we speak. Since we have only one opportunity to speak, we should do all that we can to make our words as smooth, effective, and pleasant (if needed) as possible. Here are some questions drawn from Quintilian to ask yourself before speaking:

What is the most effective way to present this speech? Should I stand? Deliver it while seated? Where in the room should I position myself?

What sections should I emphasize? Do some portions of the speech need to be delivered slowly, and others quickly? And if so, which ones?

Of the *delivery*, Quintilian writes:

Whenever [the speaker] has to raise his voice, the effort may be that of his lungs, and not of his head, and that his gesture may be suited to his looks, and his looks to his gesture. [The teacher] will have to take care, also, that the face of his pupil, while speaking, look straight forward; that his lips be not distorted; that no opening of the mouth immoderately distend his jaws; and that his face be not turned up, or his eyes cast down too much or his head inclined [too much] to either side. The face offends in various ways: I have seen many speakers whose eye-brows were raised at every effort of the voice; those of others I have seen contracted; and those of some even disagreeing, as they turned up one towards the top of the head, while with the other eye itself was almost concealed. To all these matters, as we shall hereafter show, a vast deal of importance is to be attached, for nothing can please which is unbecoming.

Drawing on these ancient examples and personal experience, we have included seven practical tips for public speaking.

Memorizing Your Speech

Memorizing Your Speech: As we noted in the previous chapter, memorizing a speech will help in the delivery of that speech. While you may not have the time to fully memorize your speech, practice reciting your speech multiple times or keep an outline in front of you, to help in moving effectively from one section to another.

Protecting your Voice: If your vocal cords become strained, it can affect the sound and quality of your voice. Consider the following tips:

Avoid the extremes of your voice like whispering and screaming, both of which can harm your vocal cords.

Rest, particularly when you are sick, and exercise to help increase your stamina.

Drink lots of water, which helps your vocal cords stay healthy, almost like rosin for a violin bow.

Avoid drinks with caffeine and even spicy foods prior to giving your speech, which can dry out your vocal cords.

Eye Contact: If you can periodically make eye contact with the audience, this tactic will help improve the overall effectiveness of your speech. Generally, you do not want to make eye contact with a single person out there in the audience; instead, look over the heads of the people you are addressing so that it looks like you are addressing the whole audience, not a single individual. Divide the audience up into three groups—the left side of the room, the right side of the room, and the middle. Then, make a conscious effort to look at each group while you speak.

Avoid Verbal Clutter: Verbal clutter is your mind's attempt to figure out what you should say next. Instead of using a filler word such as "like" or "um", simply pause, and try to time these meaningful pauses so that they come into appropriate parts of your speech: at the end of a significant point, after a powerful statistic, etc. This pause also gives your audience time to process what you have said and makes you sound in control of your speech.

Voice Volume: Projecting your voice helps your words and ideas be heard over a larger area and a wider audience. With microphones and other elements of modern sound equipment, voice volume does not seem

According to legend, Demosthenes practiced his speeches in front of the roaring ocean to improve his ability to project his voice.

so important. But, every once in a while, microphones go out or you are speaking in a location without speakers and amplifiers. On such occasions, you will be happy you worked on projecting your voice.

To project your voice, speak from the space between your lungs known as the *diaphragm*. Your diaphragm is a muscle that helps your lungs expand and inflate with air. If you can practice speaking from your diaphragm and not from the back of your throat, your voice will sound considerably deeper and louder.

Mannerisms & Posture: Even though you are speaking, what you do with your hands and your posture still matters for the delivery and the reception of your speech. For posture, be sure to stand up straight and try to project an aura of confidence and surety. Try to keep from slouching your shoulders or slumping over the podium. Your audience is more likely to believe your words if you carry yourself with a degree of authority and self-confidence, both of which are projected by standing up straight. Hand motions can be very distracting and hurt the way you appear to your audience, so be careful with what you do with your hands while you speak. Avoid the extremes of keeping your hands in your pockets versus waving your hands. Do not wring your hands or hook your thumbs on anything unless such a gesture is intentional. On the whole, keep your hands calm and composed. You can use hand motions to emphasize a point, but you should practice these moments in order to increase their overall effectiveness.

Nervousness: We all get nervous before a speech. Many people even list public speaking as their number one fear. The key is to accept you may be nervous and you may mispronounce a word or two, but you are going to try your best. Moreover, you will deliver a speech that also exhorts your listeners towards some good and noble endeavor, whatever that may look like. To help get over nervousness, consider practicing your speech in front of some friends or even a mirror. That will help you be less nervous and get over any initial fears and anxieties you may have before speaking.

Practically, we should strive to make eye contact with our audience. We should deliver our speech with appropriate voice volume—loud enough to be heard, but not too loud, and we should be aware of our hand movements to avoid distracting our audience. We should also treat our voice like a musical instrument and take care of it, eating the right foods before a speech so that we do not strain our vocal cords. Lastly, we should accept that we will be nervous and practice our speech in front of friends or a mirror. That way, we will be more confident and natural when we speak in front of a much larger group. And, if that first speech does not go well, seek out the next opportunity to give a speech and try again. In conclusion, the *pronuntiatio* refers to the delivery of your speech. In many ways, the *pronuntiatio* is the most difficult of the five canons to master. People of all ages find public speaking to be a scary endeavor because of the opportunity to look foolish in front of a large crowd of people. Thankfully, learning the five canons of rhetoric and the skills needed to compose a stirring speech can help students overcome these difficulties and become a great public speaker. Moreover, the examples of individuals like Winston Churchill, who had a speech impediment in his youth he had to overcome, and of Demosthenes, who was ridiculed after his first public speech, should give us confidence that we, too, can become great public speakers.

BIG IDEA

Public speaking is a skill like any other and with practice, one can overcome any perceived handicap. The examples of orators like Demosthenes and Winston Churchill demonstrate that an individual, driven by the desire to lead and shape public discourse for the better, can overcome such challenges and that they will be far better public speakers for their effort and hard work.

What was the best public speaking tip you gleaned from the writings of Quintilian and the example of Demosthenes? Explain why such a tip would be most helpful to you.

What was the best, most helpful, and most applicable of the seven public speaking tips presented on the previous pages? Explain your answer.

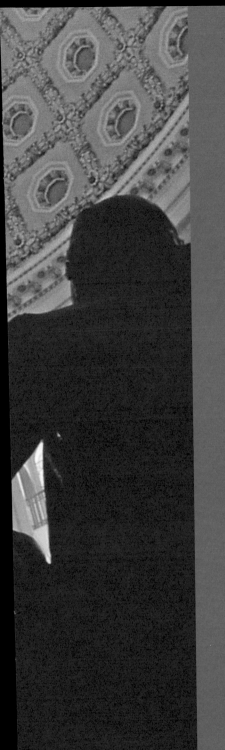

Section II
Appeals & Discourse

CHAPTER

Appeal to *Logos*

ROADMAP

✦ Learn about Aristotle's *Rhetoric* and the *Three Modes of Persuasion*.

✦ Learn how to adapt your speech and your delivery to your audience.

✦ Learn about appeals to reason or *logos*.

✦ Read selections from Patrick Henry's *Give Me Liberty* and Ronald Reagan's *A Time for Choosing*.

THALES
OUTCOME

№ 4

A Truth Seeker *critiques a variety of truth statements and/or observations through research and scientific methodology.*

As a teacher of rhetoric, Quintilian's goal was *to form, then, the perfect orator, who cannot exist unless as a good man, and we require in him, therefore, not only consummate ability in speaking, but every excellence of mind (On the Education of an Orator).* The phrase *every excellence of mind* includes not only the gifts of public speaking but also a commitment to truth telling and personal integrity.

Appeals to Logos

THE *INVENTIO* IS PERHAPS the most important of the Five Canons. The word *inventio* bears a purposeful resemblance to our English word *invention*, for the *inventio* is the *invention* or the discovery not only of the main idea of your speech—the ideas you want to advance in speaking—but also the best means to argue for that idea. Now, you may wonder, "How do I know what is the best way to argue for my position?" Thankfully, ancient teachers of rhetoric, notably the philosopher Aristotle, spent time reflecting on that question, too. As a resident in Athens, Aristotle spent countless hours in the Athenian assembly, listening to speeches and reflecting on what made certain speeches both persuasive and effective. Aristotle saw that the most effective orators knew their audience and saw, instinctively, how to persuade the audience to take up *their* policy, *their* course of action, or *their* values outlined in the speech. Aristotle boiled all the ways one could argue in support of an idea down to three broad, overarching *modes of persuasion*: logos, ethos, and pathos. In *Rhetoric*, Aristotle writes:

> *The spoken word furnishes three different modes of persuasion. The first kind depends on the personal character of the speaker (in Greek, ethos); the second on putting the audience into a certain frame of mind (in Greek, pathos); the third on the proof, or apparent proof, provided by the words of the speech itself (in Greek, logos).*

We will start our examination of **the three modes of persuasion** with an in-depth look at **logos**. Logos, the source of our English word *logic* and *logical*, refers to the use of, and appeal to, rational arguments. In short, an appeal to logos aims at moving the audience by appealing to their reason. But what kind of arguments are rational?

Aristotle says an appeal to logos can come through either arguments or examples. In other words, an appeal to logos will be a use of **deductive** or **inductive** reasoning, the kind of reasoning we have studied elsewhere in this book. An appeal to logos could include syllogisms, but, more likely, speeches will include **enthymemes**. An enthymeme is a special type of syllogism that omits or *keeps in mind* one premise. Enthymemes are to rhetoric what syllogisms are to deductive logic. Enthymemes lack the formal, three-proposition and three-term structure of a syllogism. In that way, enthymemes sound more natural than syllogisms.

Aristotle says that *examples* are the second kind of appeal to logos. By *example*, Aristotle means the use of facts, statistics, precedents, or historical analogies in making such an appeal. To illustrate this idea, Aristotle cites the likely scenario that Persia will invade Greece soon because Persia has recently invaded Egypt. By way of historical precedent, whenever Persia invaded Egypt, they invaded Greece soon after. An Athenian orator could convince the Athenian assembly a Persian invasion was likely because Persia had recently invaded Egypt, and such an event was always a prelude to war. In summary, an appeal to logos includes the use of formal argumentation, particularly in the form

Vocabulary

Write down this vocabulary in your notebook. These terms will help you better learn and understand the material in this chapter.

The Three Modes of Persuasion
The Greek philosopher Aristotle identified three different ways or modes of persuasion; they include *ethos*, *logos*, and *pathos*.

Logos
The appeal to reasoned argumentation.

Pathos
The appeal to the emotions.

Ethos
The appeal to your reputation and also how likable you are while you are speaking.

Deductive Reasoning
A form of reasoning that goes from premises to a conclusion; these arguments focus more on the form and the structure of arguments, arguments that are often expressed in the form of a syllogism.

Inductive Reasoning
A form of reasoning that goes from observations to broad, universal principles; these arguments depend more on content and evidence than on form or structure.

Enthymeme
A syllogism with one premise omitted or kept in mind; these are especially important in rhetoric.

ARISTOTLE / 384 - 322 BC

Greek philosopher and author of Rhetoric

of enthymemes, as well as examples to support the overarching point of a speech or some other piece of written communication.

As student-orators, we have to find arguments that work. Cicero, in *On the Character of the Orator*, explains his thought process behind choosing various arguments when he was speaking in public. For example, if an argument "depended on the conciliation or excitement of the feelings of the judges, I [Cicero] apply myself chiefly to that part which is best adapted to men's minds," (170). Such an argument could be an appeal to a straightforward legal principle that applies in this scenario. On the other hand, if the orator addresses a large crowd deliberating on some important subject, he or she may wish to employ more (but not too many more) arguments to win over a larger percentage of the crowd. Such arguments may include statistics or moving historical examples.

The orator may recognize that the best means of winning his or her argument resides in refuting the argument of their opponents: "if my speech can be made more effective by refuting my adversary, than by supporting my own side of the question, I employ all my weapons against him," (170). An orator must be both intellectually flexible and confident to know what strategy to employ and when—and such confidence comes through practice in actually debating. Lastly, Cicero urges the student-orator to read and study widely so as to avail him or herself of the nuanced argumentation best suited to the occasion.

Appeal to Logos

Instructions: Read over the following examples of various appeals to logic and reason. In the space provided, identify whether or not they are deductive arguments, such as an enthymeme, or examples.

Example: In the past, Persia has invaded Egypt just before they have invaded Greece. Persia just invaded Egypt, so we can assume they are preparing to invade Greece.

Using an appeal to reason through *examples*, the speaker cites one example of Persia invading Greece.

1. I want to manage my time better: since managing my time requires keeping a calendar and a routine, I will look over my calendar every week and stick to a schedule everyday.

....

....

2. The ancient world valued rhetoric because they saw it helped leaders be successful.

....

....

3. Working hard and saving your money is the key to success in life, as the examples of Benjamin Franklin and Calvin Coolidge demonstrate.

....

....

4. If you take a moment to clear your mind, you will make better decisions.

....

....

ACTIVITY

Appeal to Logos

Instructions: Read over the following examples of various appeals to logic and reason. In the space provided, identify whether or not they are logical arguments, such as an enthymeme, or examples.

5. I want to get more exercise, and since I will be more likely to exercise if I have equipment near my desk, I will keep a pair of dumbbells next to my desk.

6. James Madison and James Monroe were classically-educated, so a classical education must be integral to one's success.

7. Many of the most successful businessmen dropped out of college, so I should drop out of college, too (note: be careful of the false analogy).

8. Persia invaded Egypt before they invaded Greece because they needed to gain the funds needed to pay soldiers, ships, sailors, and supplies for a long invasion of Greece.

CHAPTER 05 Appeal to Logos + 51

Rhetorical Analysis / Instructions

The phrase *Rhetorical Analysis* refers to the careful analysis of a speech for its overall effectiveness. That is, how effective was the speaker in moving the audience to his or her goal through careful uses of appeals to *logos*, *ethos*, and *pathos*.

In the remaining chapters, we will read speeches from some of the most noteworthy orators in American history including the likes of Patrick Henry, Frederick Douglass, Ronald Reagan, Martin Luther King Jr., and John F. Kennedy. Two exercises will follow each speech to help you evaluate how effective (or ineffective) the speaker was in advancing his particular goal. These elements are explained in further detail below.

Elements for Rhetorical Analysis	Questions to Consider
Purpose, Audience, & Tone *Purpose*: The goal the speaker has in mind for their speech and what they hope to accomplish. *Audience*: The people listening to the speech and their expectations. *Tone*: The feelings the speaker has toward his subject.	*What is that goal?* *Who is their audience, and how are they likely to feel about that goal?* *How does the speaker feel about that particular goal?*
The Means of Persuasion & Appeals to Logos, Ethos, & Pathos *Logos*: An appeal to reasoned argumentation. *Ethos*: Not only your reputation but also how likable you are while you are speaking. *Pathos*: An appeal to the emotions.	*Does the speaker make an argument? If so, If so, how does it make the speech more (or less) effective?* *Does he appeal to an emotion? If so, what emotion, and why that emotion and not another?* *Does the speaker make reference to his or her own character? If so, how does it make the speech more (or less) effective?*

Rhetorical Analysis / Liberty or Death

Instructions: Identify appeals to logos in Patrick Henry's *Give Me Liberty Or Give Me Death*, delivered on March 23, 1775.

Patrick Henry ranks amongst the best and most eloquent orators in colonial America. He is most famous for the speech we provide here for your analysis, *Give Me Liberty Or Give Me Death*, delivered before the members at the Second Virginia Convention at St. John's Episcopal Church in Richmond, Virginia. At the time, the Royal Navy was blockading the port of Boston, and King George III was taking other steps to stifle the spirit of revolution in the American colonies. The Virginia delegates at St. John's Episcopal had to decide whether they would submit to British authority and rule, and Henry hoped to persuade them to risk everything for the cause of independence.

March 23, 1775

No man thinks more highly than I do of the patriotism, as well as abilities, of the very worthy gentlemen who have just addressed the House. But different men often see the same subject in different lights; and, therefore, I hope it will not be thought disrespectful to those gentlemen if, entertaining as I do opinions of a character very opposite to theirs, I shall speak forth my sentiments freely and without reserve. This is no time for ceremony. The question before the House is one of awful moment to this country. For my own part, I consider it as nothing less than a question of freedom or slavery; and in proportion to the magnitude of the subject ought to be the freedom of the debate. It is only in this way that we can hope to arrive at truth, and fulfill the great responsibility which we hold to God and our country. Should I keep back my opinions at such a time, through fear of giving offense, I should consider myself as guilty of treason towards my country, and of an act of disloyalty toward the Majesty of Heaven, which I revere above all earthly kings.

Mr. President, it is natural to man to indulge in the illusions of hope. We are apt to shut our eyes against a painful truth, and listen to the song of that siren till she transforms us into beasts. Is this the part of wise men, engaged in a great and arduous struggle for liberty? Are we disposed to be of the number of those who, having eyes, see not, and, having ears, hear not, the things which so nearly concern their temporal salvation? For my part, whatever anguish of spirit it may cost, I am willing to know the whole truth; to know the worst, and to provide for it.

I have but one lamp by which my feet are guided, and that is the lamp of experience. I know of no way of judging of the future but by the past. And judging by the past, I wish to know what there has been in the conduct of the British ministry for the last ten years to justify those hopes with which gentlemen have been pleased to solace themselves and the House. Is it that insidious smile with which our petition has been lately received? Trust it not, sir; it will prove a snare to your feet. Suffer not yourselves to be betrayed with a kiss. Ask yourselves how this gracious reception of our petition comports with those warlike preparations which cover our waters and darken our land. Are fleets and armies necessary to a work of love and reconciliation? Have we shown ourselves so unwilling to be reconciled that force must be called in to win back our love? Let us not deceive ourselves, sir. These are the implements of war and subjugation; the last arguments to which kings resort. I ask gentlemen, sir, what means this martial array, if its purpose be not to force us to submission? Can gentlemen assign any other possible motive for it?

Has Great Britain any enemy, in this quarter of the world, to call for all this accumulation of navies and armies? No, sir, she has none. They are meant for us: they can be meant for no other. They are sent over to bind and rivet upon us those chains which the British ministry have been so long forging. And what have we to oppose to them? Shall we try argument? Sir, we have been trying that for the last ten years. Have we anything new to offer upon the subject? Nothing. We have held the subject up in every light of which it is capable; but it has been all in vain. Shall we resort to entreaty and humble supplication? What terms shall we find which have not been already exhausted? Let us not, I beseech you, sir, deceive ourselves. Sir, we have done everything that could be done to avert the storm which is now coming on.

We have petitioned; we have remonstrated; we have supplicated; we have prostrated ourselves before the throne, and have implored its interposition to arrest the tyrannical hands of the ministry and Parliament. Our petitions have been slighted; our remonstrances have produced additional violence and insult; our supplications have been disregarded; and we have been spurned, with contempt, from the foot of the throne! In vain, after these things, may we indulge the fond hope of peace and reconciliation. There is no longer any room for hope. If we wish to be free—if we mean to preserve inviolate those inestimable privileges for which we have been so long contending—if we mean not basely to abandon the noble struggle in which we have been so long engaged, and which we have pledged ourselves never to abandon until the glorious object of our contest shall be obtained—we must fight! I repeat it, sir, we must fight! An appeal to arms and to the God of hosts is all that is left us!

They tell us, sir, that we are weak; unable to cope with so formidable an adversary. But when shall we be stronger? Will it be the next week, or the next year? Will it be when we are totally disarmed, and when a British guard shall be stationed in every house? Shall we gather strength by irresolution and inaction? Shall we acquire the means of effectual resistance by lying supinely on our backs and hugging the delusive phantom of hope, until our enemies shall have bound us hand and foot? Sir, we are not weak if we make a proper use of those means which the God of nature hath placed in our power. The millions of people, armed in the holy cause of liberty, and in such a country as that which we possess, are invincible by any force which our enemy can send against us. Besides, sir, we shall not fight our battles alone. There is a just God who presides over the destinies of nations, and who will raise up friends to fight our battles for us. The battle, sir, is not to the strong alone; it is to the vigilant, the active, the brave. Besides, sir, we have no election. If we were base enough to desire it, it is now too late to retire from the contest. There is no retreat but in submission and slavery! Our chains are forged! Their clanking may be heard on the plains of Boston! The war is inevitable—and let it come! I repeat it, sir, let it come.

It is in vain, sir, to extenuate the matter. Gentlemen may cry, *Peace, Peace*—but there is no peace. The war is actually begun! The next gale that sweeps from the north will bring to our ears the clash of resounding arms! Our brethren are already in the field! Why stand we here idle? What is it that gentlemen wish? What would they have? Is life so dear, or peace so sweet, as to be purchased at the price of chains and slavery? Forbid it, Almighty God! I know not what course others may take; but as for me, give me liberty or give me death!

Rhetorical Analysis / **Give me Liberty!**

Instructions: In the space provided, answer the following questions concerning the purpose, audience, and tone of the speech to help you identify rhetorical appeals. Answer in complete sentences.

Criteria	*Description*
The Purpose of the Speech *Why did the orator deliver this speech? What was his goal?*	
The Audience of the Speech *Who was the audience? What was the occasion?*	
The Tone of the Speech *Tone is the way that an orator or an author feels about his work and the subject at hand.* *How does the speaker feel about the subject he is speaking about?*	

Rhetorical Analysis / Give me Liberty!

Instructions: In the table below, we have provided a number of quotations from the speech, each of which makes an *appeal to logos*. Read over the quote and summarize the *appeal to logos* being made by the speaker. How does it help prove or support the speaker's argument?

Quotation	Description
Has Great Britain any enemy, in this quarter of the world, to call for all this accumulation of navies and armies? No, sir, she has none. They are meant for us: they can be meant for no other. They are sent over to bind and rivet upon us those chains which the British ministry have been so long forging.	
They tell us, sir, that we are weak; unable to cope with so formidable an adversary. But when shall we be stronger? ...millions of people, armed in the holy cause of liberty, and in such a country as that which we possess, are invincible by any force which our enemy can send against us.	
Our brethren are already in the field! Why stand we here idle? What is it that gentlemen wish? What would they have? Is life so dear, or peace so sweet, as to be purchased at the price of chains and slavery? Forbid it, Almighty God! I know not what course others may take; but as for me, give me liberty or give me death!	

Rhetorical Analysis / A Time for Choosing

Instructions: Identify appeals to logos in Ronald Reagan's *A Time for Choosing*, delivered on October 27, 1964.

Ronald Reagan began his career as an actor and, at times, it shows. On October 27, 1964, Reagan spoke before a crowd of Republican Party officials urging them to support the candidacy of Arizona Senator Barry Goldwater. Goldwater ran on a platform of rolling back government programs enacted by President Lyndon Johnson as part of Johnson's Great Society; Johnson touted these government programs as part of an all-out war on poverty.

But, as Reagan demonstrates in this speech, the "facts" behind these programs do not add up. Aristotle lists two different ways of employing an attempt at logos: syllogisms and examples. This particular speech provides multiple examples in the form of statistics to help, in part, prove Reagan's point about the unnecessary intrusion of government programs into private life and the unintended consequences that arise when such programs are enacted.

October 27, 1964

Thank you. Thank you very much. Thank you and good evening. The sponsor has been identified, but unlike most television programs, the performer hasn't been provided with a script. As a matter of fact, I have been permitted to choose my own words and discuss my own ideas regarding the choice that we face in the next few weeks.

I have spent most of my life as a Democrat. I recently have seen fit to follow another course. I believe that the issues confronting us cross party lines. Now, one side in this campaign has been telling us that the issues of this

‖ RONALD REAGAN / 1911 - 2004

election are the maintenance of peace and prosperity. The line has been used, "We've never had it so good."

But I have an uncomfortable feeling that this prosperity isn't something on which we can base our hopes for the future. No nation in history has ever survived a tax burden that reached a third of its national income. Today, 37 cents out of every dollar earned in this country is the tax collector's share, and yet our government continues to spend 17 million dollars a day more than the government takes in. We haven't balanced our budget 28 out of the last 34 years.

We've raised our debt limit three times in the last twelve months, and now our national debt is one and a half times bigger than all the combined debts of all the nations of the world. We have 15 billion dollars in gold in our treasury; we don't own an ounce. Foreign dollar claims are 27.3 billion dollars. And we've just had announced that the dollar of 1939 will now purchase 45 cents in its total value.

As for the peace that we would preserve, I wonder who among us would like to approach the wife or mother whose husband or son has died in South Vietnam and ask them if they think this is a peace that should be maintained indefinitely. Do they mean peace, or do they mean we just want to be left in peace? There can be no real peace while one American is dying some place in the world for the rest of us. We're at war with the most dangerous enemy that has ever faced mankind in his long climb from the swamp to the stars, and it's been said if we lose that war, and in so doing lose this way of freedom of ours, history will record with the greatest astonishment that those who had the most to lose did the least to prevent its happening. Well I think it's time we ask ourselves if we still know the freedoms that were intended for us by the Founding Fathers.

Not too long ago, two friends of mine were talking to a Cuban refugee, a businessman who had escaped from Castro, and in the midst of his story one of my friends turned to the other and said, "We don't know how lucky we are." And the Cuban stopped and said, "How lucky you are? I had someplace to escape to." And in that sentence he told us the entire story. If we lose freedom here, there's no place to escape to. This is the last stand on earth.

And this idea that government is beholden to the people, that it has no other source of power except the sovereign people, is still the newest and the most unique idea in all the long history of man's relation to man.

This is the issue of this election: Whether we believe in our capacity for self-government or whether we abandon the American revolution and confess that a little intellectual elite in a far-distant capitol can plan our lives for us better than we can plan them ourselves.

You and I are told increasingly we have to choose between a left or right. Well I'd like to suggest there is no such thing as a left or right. There's only an up or down - [up] man's old-aged dream, the ultimate in individual freedom consistent with law and order, or down to the ant heap of totalitarianism. And regardless of their sincerity, their humanitarian motives, those who would trade our freedom for security have embarked on this downward course.

In this vote-harvesting time, they use terms like the "Great Society", or as we were told a few days ago by the President, we must accept a greater government activity in the affairs of the people. But they've been a little more explicit in the past and among themselves; and all of the things I now will quote have appeared in print. These are not Republican accusations. For example, they have voices that say, "The cold war will end through our acceptance of a not undemocratic socialism." Another voice says, "The profit motive has become outmoded. It must be replaced by the incentives of the welfare state." Or, "Our traditional system of individual freedom is incapable of solving the complex problems of the 20th century." Senator Fullbright has said at Stanford University that the Constitution is outmoded. He referred to the President as "our moral teacher and our leader," and he says he is "hobbled in his task by the restrictions of power imposed on him by this antiquated document." He must "be freed," so that he "can do for us" what he knows "is best." And Senator Clark of Pennsylvania, another articulate spokesman, defines liberalism as "meeting the material needs of the masses through the full power of centralized government."

Well, I, for one, resent it when a representative of the people refers to you and me, the free men and women of this country, as "the masses." This is a term we haven't applied to ourselves in America. But beyond that, "the full power of centralized government", this was the very thing the Founding Fathers sought to minimize.

They knew that governments don't control things. A government can't control the economy without controlling people. And they know when a government sets out to do that, it must use force and coercion to achieve its purpose. They also knew, those Founding Fathers, that outside of its legitimate functions, government does nothing as well or as economically as the private sector of the economy.

Now, we have no better example of this than government's involvement in the farm economy over the last 30 years. Since 1955, the cost of this program has nearly doubled. One-fourth of farming in America is responsible for 85 percent of the farm surplus. Three-fourths of farming is out on the free market and has known a 21 percent increase in the per capita consumption of all its produce. You see, that one-fourth of farming that's regulated and controlled by the federal government. In the last three years we've spent 43 dollars in the feed grain program for every dollar bushel of corn we don't grow.

Senator Humphrey last week charged that Barry Goldwater, as President, would seek to eliminate farmers. He should do his homework a little better, because he'll find out that we've had a decline of 5 million in the farm population under these government programs. He'll also find that the Democratic administration has sought to get from Congress [an] extension of the farm program to include that three-fourths that is now free. He'll find that they've also asked for the right to imprison farmers who wouldn't keep books as prescribed by the federal government. The Secretary of Agriculture asked for the right to seize farms through condemnation and resell them to other individuals. And contained in that same program was a provision that would have allowed the federal government to remove 2 million farmers from the soil.

At the same time, there's been an increase in the Department of Agriculture employees. There's now one for every 30 farms in the United States, and still they can't tell us how 66 shiploads of grain headed for Austria disappeared without a trace and Billie Sol Estes never left shore.

Every responsible farmer and farm organization has repeatedly asked the government to free the farm economy, but how - who are farmers to know what's best for them? The wheat farmers voted against a wheat program. The government passed it anyway. Now the price of bread goes up; the price of wheat to the farmer goes down.

Meanwhile, back in the city, under urban renewal the assault on freedom carries on. Private property rights [are] so diluted that public interest is almost anything a few government planners decide it should be. In a program that takes from the needy and gives to the greedy, we see such spectacles as in Cleveland, Ohio, a million-and-a-half-dollar building completed only three years ago must be destroyed to make way for what government officials call a "more compatible use of the land." The President tells us he's now going to start building public housing units in the thousands, where heretofore we've only built them in the hundreds. But FHA [Federal Housing Authority] and the Veterans Administration tell us they have 120,000 housing units they've taken back through mortgage foreclosure. For three decades, we've sought to solve the problems of unemployment through government planning, and the more the plans fail, the more the planners plan. The latest is the Area Redevelopment Agency.

They've just declared Rice County, Kansas, a depressed area. Rice County, Kansas, has two hundred oil wells, and the 14,000 people there have over 30 million dollars on deposit in personal savings in their banks.

And when the government tells you you're depressed, lie down and be depressed.

We have so many people who can't see a fat man standing beside a thin one without coming to the conclusion the fat man got that way by taking advantage of the thin one. So they're going to solve all the problems of human misery through government and government planning. Well, now, if government planning and welfare had the answer - and they've had almost 30 years of it - shouldn't we expect government to read the score to us once in a while? Shouldn't they be telling us about the decline each year in the number of people needing help? The reduction in the need for public housing?

But the reverse is true. Each year the need grows greater; the program grows greater. We were told four years ago that 17 million people went to bed hungry each night. Well that was probably true. They were all on a diet. But now we're told that 9.3 million families in this country are poverty-stricken on the basis of earning less than 3,000 dollars a year. Welfare spending [is] 10 times greater than in the dark depths of the Depression. We're spending 45 billion dollars on welfare. Now do a little arithmetic, and you'll find that if we divided the 45 billion dollars up equally among those 9 million poor families, we'd be able to give each family 4,600 dollars a year. And this added to their present income should eliminate poverty. Direct aid to the poor, however, is only running only about 600 dollars per family. It would seem that someplace there must be some overhead.

Now, so now we declare "war on poverty," or "You, too, can be a Bobby Baker." Now do they honestly expect us to believe that if we add 1 billion dollars to the 45 billion we're spending, one more program to the 30-odd we have -and remember, this new program doesn't replace any, it just duplicates existing programs - do they believe that poverty is suddenly going to disappear by magic? Well, in all fairness I should explain there is one part of the new program that isn't duplicated. This is the youth feature. We're now going to solve the dropout problem, juvenile delinquency, by reinstituting something like the old CCC camps [Civilian Conservation Corps], and we're going to put our young people in these camps. But again we do some arithmetic, and we find that we're going to spend each year just on room and board for each young person we help 4,700 dollars a year. We can send them to Harvard for 2,700! Course, don't get me wrong. I'm not suggesting Harvard is the answer to juvenile delinquency.

But seriously, what are we doing to those we seek to help?

Rhetorical Analysis / A Time for Choosing

Instructions: In the space provided, answer the following questions concerning the purpose, audience, and tone of the speech to help you identify rhetorical appeals. Answer in complete sentences.

Criteria	Description
The Purpose of the Speech *Why did the orator deliver this speech? What was his goal?*	
The Audience of the Speech *Who was the audience? What was the occasion?*	
The Tone of the Speech *Tone is the way that an orator or an author feels about his work and the subject at hand.* *How does the speaker feel about the subject he is speaking about?*	

Rhetorical Analysis / A Time for Choosing

Instructions: Read over the quotations below from the speech, each of which makes an *appeal to logos*. Read over the quotation and summarize the *appeal to logos* being made by the speaker. How does it help prove or support the speaker's argument?

Quotation	Description
Senator Humphrey [Lyndon Johnson's Vice President and running mate] last week charged that Barry Goldwater, as President, would seek to eliminate farmers. He should do his homework a little better, because he'll find out that we've had a decline of 5 million in the farm population under these government programs.	
The President tells us he's now going to start building public housing units in the thousands, where heretofore we've only built them in the hundreds. But FHA [Federal Housing Authority] and the Veterans Administration tell us they have 120,000 housing units they've taken back through mortgage foreclosure. For three decades, we've sought to solve the problems of unemployment through government planning, and the more the plans fail, the more the planners plan.	
But now we're told that 9.3 million families in this country are poverty-stricken on the basis of earning less than 3,000 dollars a year. Welfare spending [is] 10 times greater than in the dark depths of the Depression. We're spending 45 billion dollars on welfare. Now do a little arithmetic, and you'll find that if we divided the 45 billion dollars up equally among those 9 million poor families, we'd be able to give each family 4,600 dollars a year. And this added to their present income should eliminate poverty. Direct aid to the poor, however, is only running only about 600 dollars per family. It would seem that someplace there must be some overhead.	

As far as appeals to logos, did Patrick Henry use more logical arguments or more examples? How effective were they? Explain your reasoning.

As far as appeals to logos, did Ronald Reagan use more logical arguments or more examples? How effective were they? Explain your reasoning.

Canon of Memory / Give me Liberty!

Of the five canons, the canon of *memoria* may be the hardest canon to master. The practice of memorizing a speech requires considerable time and effort, but, like any skill, memorizing a speech becomes easier and easier the more things you try to memorize. We can use select speeches (like the one we just read) to practice our ability to memorize important passages and learn one method by which we can begin to memorize longer blocks of text. That method is to memorize one clause or sentence at a time, and then to go back and repeat *all of the sentences* you've memorized until you can recite the entire passage from memory.

> *It is in vain, sir, to extenuate the matter. Gentlemen may cry, Peace, Peace—but there is no peace. The war is actually begun! The next gale that sweeps from the north will bring to our ears the clash of resounding arms! Our brethren are already in the field! Why stand we here idle? What is it that gentlemen wish? What would they have? Is life so dear, or peace so sweet, as to be purchased at the price of chains and slavery? Forbid it, Almighty God! I know not what course others may take; but as for me, give me liberty or give me death!*

Step and Description	Lines from Patrick Henry's Speech
Step 1: Read the first clause or sentence out loud upwards of five to ten times. Try to recite the sentence without looking at the words.	*It is in vain, sir, to extenuate the matter…*
Step 2: Read the next clause or sentence out loud upwards of five to ten times. Try to recite the sentence without looking at the words.	*Gentlemen may cry, Peace, Peace—but there is no peace…*
Step 3: Go back to the beginning and repeat the first two clauses or sentences. Repeat until you have memorized the passage in question.	*It is in vain, sir, to extenuate the matter… Gentlemen may cry, Peace, Peace—but there is no peace…*
Suggested Assignment: Recite the speech from memory for a homework, classwork, or assessment grade with one point for each word memorized (may also be taken as a percentage).	_____ / 106 points

Writing Prompt

In the space provided, what was the most valuable concept or idea you learned about in this chapter? Why *that* idea or concept, and not another? If you have had opportunities to speak in public before, how might have the material in this chapter helped you? Reflect, too, on the speech(es) provided in this chapter: why did the ideas and goals communicated in the speech matter, and how did the speaker go about trying to persuade the audience to believe in them?

06

CHAPTER

Appeals to *Ethos*

ROADMAP

✦ Review Aristotle's *Rhetoric* and the *Three Modes of Persuasion*.

✦ Learn about appeals to *ethos* and how to frame an appeal to *ethos*.

✦ Read selections from Frederick Douglass' *What to the Slave is the Fourth of July?*

THALES
OUTCOME

№ 5

A **Critical Thinker** *analyzes a variety of truth statements and/or observations through a dialectic examination of facts and assumptions.*

An appeal to *ethos* is the appeal to and from the character of the speaker. If an orator can correctly read his audience and understand their needs, the orator can adjust his speech accordingly to best meet those needs. Such an approach requires quick, critical thinking to make such choices so quickly.

Appeals to Ethos

THE RHETORICAL TRIANGLE of *logos, ethos,* and *pathos* is a helpful and useful strategy for composing and delivering a speech. Once you know your audience and the best way to reach them, an appeal to *logos, ethos,* or *pathos* fall into place easier. We covered the appeal to *logos* in the previous chapter; now, let's turn to the appeal to *ethos.*

The appeal to *ethos* is the appeal from the character of the speaker. In the *Rhetoric,* Aristotle states an orator must take care that "his own character look right... [and] that the orator's own character should look right is particularly important in political speaking," (59). Subsequently, an appeal to *ethos* may involve sounding and appearing professional, courteous, and well-mannered, even friendly. That appearance depends on the audience the orator addresses. An orator may want to dress in a suit and tie if his audience is most likely wearing a suit and tie, or appear in (nice) jeans if the audience is younger and more casual—such concerns depend on context. An appeal to *ethos* may also include the expertise of the speaker, their credentials, and their personal reputation.

Ethos often involves how likable the speaker is during the speech. That is, an appeal to and from *ethos* may involve how likable and personable the speaker is since an audience is likely to make quick judgments of the speaker's ability in the first few minutes of a speech. A famous example of *ethos* in action was the first televised presidential debate in the United States which took place between John F. Kennedy and Richard M. Nixon. Many people who listened to the debate over the radio believed Nixon won, whereas those who watched the debate on television believed

Kennedy was the winner. Nixon may have sounded more impressive, but Kennedy's charisma and personal demeanor made him appear the superior candidate. To those who watched the debate on television, Kennedy won based on his superior appeal to and from *ethos.* Here, the words of Cicero prove particularly helpful: "A [playful or humorous] manner, too, and strokes of wit, give pleasure to an audience, and are often of great advantage to the speaker," (144). We have provided a sample exercise at the end of this chapter based on the Kennedy-Nixon debates so that you can decide for yourself who made the better appeal to *ethos.*

Aristotle in his *Rhetoric* writes that an orator "must also make his own character right," (59). This statement does not mean that an orator should change his character or his convictions to suit his audience—that would be dishonest. If an orator who is a graduate of UNC Chapel Hill addresses an audience of NC State fans, that orator should not pretend to like NC State. That would not only be dishonest but also counterproductive, for the audience would lose all confidence in the orator once they discovered the trick (In this case, perhaps, the orator should appeal only to their shared rivalry with Duke if they speak about college rivalries at all). In this case, the orator should be careful to consider the needs and composition of their audience. That way, when they address that crowd, their audience does not reject their arguments based on something arbitrary they see or hear in the speaker.

As a result, the orator should take steps to "inspire confidence in [his or her] own character." Aristotle lists three ways that the orator may inspire such confidence: "good sense, good moral character, and

Vocabulary

Write down this vocabulary in your notebook. These terms will help you better learn and understand the material in this chapter.

The Three Modes of Persuasion
The Greek philosopher Aristotle identified three different ways or modes of persuasion; they include *ethos*, *logos*, and *pathos*.

Logos
The appeal to reasoned argumentation.

Pathos
The appeal to the emotions.

Ethos
This is not only your reputation but also how likable you are while you are speaking.

RHETORIC / PIETER ISAACSZ (OR REINHOLD TIMM)
A knight lecturing in a painting, symbolizing the art of rhetoric

goodwill." An orator who demonstrates these good qualities should "inspire trust in his audience," (60). In *Rhetoric*, Aristotle treats *pathos* first, examining the emotions that the orator may stir in his or her audience. Then, Aristotle addresses the kinds of people who may be in that audience, for the goal of adapting one's speech within reasonable, moral limits to the needs of that audience. Aristotle writes, "people always think well of speeches adapted to, and reflecting, their own character: and we can now see how to compose our speeches so as to adapt both them and ourselves to our audiences," (86). First, Aristotle addresses human beings in their youth, then in their old age, and lastly in the "prime" of their life when they are neither of these things (87). An orator can frame appeals to *ethos* based off of the temperament of their audience—an audience of mostly young people may not be stirred or persuaded by the same arguments as a more elderly audience, for example.

In summary, an appeal to *ethos* is an appeal based on the character of the speaker. Such an appeal would include both their reputation and their demeanor, a demeanor that can be shaped based upon the composition of the audience. In the following pages, we have provided Aristotle's advice on the feelings and temperament of the young, the elderly, and those in their prime and how to frame an appeal to ethos. Then, on the page that immediately follows, we have provided some sample exercises to frame an ethical appeal of your own.

Appeal to Ethos

Instructions: In the table below, we have provided quotations from the *Rhetoric* on how to frame an appeal to *ethos* to each group, and what motivates each group.

Appeals to Ethos based on Age	Aristotle's Description
The Young	*Young men have strong passions, and tend to gratify them indiscriminately...they look at the good side rather than the bad, not having yet witnessed many instances of wickedness. They trust others readily, because they have not yet often been cheated...their hot tempers and hopeful dispositions make them more courageous than older men are; the hot temper prevents fear, and the hopeful disposition creates confidence.* *They have exalted notions, because they have not yet been humbled by life or [learned] its necessary limitations; moreover, their hopeful disposition makes them think themselves equal to great things—and that means having exalted notions,* (84-85).
The Elderly *Please note that a textbook example of hubris is to look down upon the elderly, as if we will not one day be old (cf. Arachne and Minerva from Ovid's* Metamorphoses*).*	*Those who "have lived many years; they have often been taken in, and often made mistakes; and life on the whole is a bad business. The result is that are sure about nothing and under-do everything. They 'think,' but they never 'know'; and because of their hesitation they always add a 'possibly' or a 'perhaps,' putting everything this way and nothing positively....[because] they have been humbled by life,"* (85).
Those in their Prime	*We shall find that they have a character between that of the young and that of the old, free from the extremes of either. They have neither that excess of confidence which amounts to rashness [in youth], nor too much timidity [as in the elderly], but the right amount of each.* *Their lives will be guided not by the sole consideration either of what is noble or of what is useful, but of both, neither by [being too generous] or [not being generous enough], but by what is fit and proper,* (87).

Appeal to Ethos

Instructions: In the table below, write a few sentences about how you would appeal to each age group, providing that your audience is overwhelmingly composed of people from that age group. A suggested reason for speaking is also included. Refer to the table on the previous page for insights.

Appeals to Ethos based on Age	Your Appeal
The Young / *Encouraging a group of high school students to get a part-time job after school.*	
The Elderly / *Encouraging a group of residents at a senior citizens rest home to come and volunteer at a local school.*	
Those in their Prime / *Encouraging a group of twenty-something young professionals to volunteer at a local soup kitchen.*	

Rhetorical Analysis / **What to the Slave is the Fourth of July**

Instructions: Identify appeals to ethos in Frederick Douglass' *What to the Slave is the Fourth of July*, delivered on July 5, 1852 in Rochester, New York.

Frederick Douglass did not know many of the details surrounding his own birth, not even his own birthday or the identity of his real father. He was born around 1817-1818 on a plantation in Talbot County, Maryland, and died in 1895. He details the traumatic experiences of his childhood in his autobiography and his efforts to gain an education whilst he was "rented out" to shipbuilders in Baltimore, Maryland. He escaped from Maryland and headed north to Philadelphia and New York and then New Bedford, Massachusetts. Upon gaining his freedom, Douglass gained a considerable reputation as an orator and public speaker, who traveled and spoke widely on behalf of the abolitionist movement in the United States. Amongst his most famous speeches is the selection included here, entitled *What to the Slave is the Fourth of July*.

Frederick Douglass had been asked by the Ladies Anti-Slavery Society of Rochester to speak on the meaning of the Declaration of Independence. The date was July 5th, 1852, a mere day after the anniversary of July 4th, the signing of the Declaration of Independence. Thus, as an enslaved person who had escaped to freedom, Douglass is in a unique position to highlight the discrepancy between the promises of freedom outlined in the Declaration of Independence and all of the freedoms that African slaves lacked, despite being made in God's image and endowed with the same *inalienable rights* promised in the Declaration. His goal in speaking is to encourage his audience to take up the cause of freedom and support the ending of slavery. So as we read, let us consider all of the ways that Frederick Douglass appeals to his audience based on his

character. What makes Frederick Douglass' speech so powerful and effective? What sorts of appeals to *ethos*, appeals based on his character, does Douglass make in this speech?

July 5, 1852

Mr. President, Friends and Fellow Citizens:

He who could address this audience without a quailing sensation, has stronger nerves than I have. I do not remember ever to have appeared as a speaker before any assembly more shrinkingly, nor with greater distrust of my ability, than I do this day. A feeling has crept over me, quite unfavorable to the exercise of my limited powers of speech. The task before me is one which requires much previous thought and study for its proper performance. I know that apologies of this sort are generally considered flat and unmeaning. I trust, however, that mine will not be so considered. Should I seem at ease, my appearance would much misrepresent me. The little experience I have had in addressing public meetings, in country schoolhouses, avails me nothing on the present occasion.

The papers and placards say, that I am to deliver a 4th [of] July oration. This certainly sounds large, and out of the common way, for it is true that I have often had the privilege to speak in this beautiful Hall, and to address many who now honor me with their presence. But neither their familiar faces, nor the perfect gage I think I have of Corinthian Hall, seems to free me from embarrassment.

The fact is, ladies and gentlemen, the distance between this platform and the slave plantation, from which I escaped, is considerable — and the difficulties to be overcome in getting from the latter to the former, are by no means slight. That I am here to-day is, to me, a matter of astonishment as well as of gratitude. You will not, therefore, be surprised, if in what I have to say I evince no elaborate preparation, nor grace my speech with any high sounding exordium [*note: an exordium is an introduction to a speech*]. With little experience and with less learning, I have been able to throw my thoughts hastily and imperfectly together; and trusting to your patient and generous indulgence, I will proceed to lay them before you.

This, for the purpose of this celebration, is the 4th of July. It is the birthday of your National Independence, and of your political freedom. This, to you, is what the Passover was to the emancipated people of God. It carries your minds back to the day, and to the act of your great deliverance; and to the signs, and to the wonders, associated with that act, and that day. This celebration also marks the beginning of another year of your national life; and reminds you that the Republic of America is now 76 years old. I am glad, fellow-citizens, that your nation is so young. Seventy-six years, though a good old age for a man, is but a mere speck in the life of a nation. Three score years and ten is the allotted time for individual men; but nations number their years by thousands. According to this fact, you are, even now, only in the beginning of your national career, still lingering in the period of childhood. I repeat, I am glad this is so. There is hope in the thought, and hope is much needed, under the dark clouds which lower above the horizon. The eye of the reformer is met with angry flashes, portending disastrous times; but his heart may well beat lighter at the thought that America is young, and that she is still in the impressible stage of her existence. May he not hope that high lessons of wisdom, of justice and of truth, will yet give direction to her destiny? Were the nation older, the patriot's heart might be sadder, and the reformer's brow heavier. Its future might be shrouded in gloom, and the hope

FREDERICK DOUGLASS / 1818 - 1895

of its prophets go out in sorrow. There is consolation in the thought that America is young. Great streams are not easily turned from channels, worn deep in the course of ages. They may sometimes rise in quiet and stately majesty, and inundate the land, refreshing and fertilizing the earth with their mysterious properties. They may also rise in wrath and fury, and bear away, on their angry waves, the accumulated wealth of years of toil and hardship. They, however, gradually flow back to the same old channel, and flow on as serenely as ever. But, while the river may not be turned aside, it may dry up, and leave nothing behind but the withered branch, and the unsightly rock, to howl in the abyss-sweeping wind, the sad tale of departed glory. As with rivers so with nations.

Fellow-citizens, I shall not presume to dwell at length on the associations that cluster about this day. The simple story of it is that, 76 years ago, the people of this country were British subjects. The style and title of your "sovereign people" (in which you now glory) was not then born. You were under the British Crown. Your fathers esteemed the English Government as the home government; and England as the fatherland. This home government, you know, although a considerable distance from your home, did, in the exercise of its parental prerogatives, impose upon its colonial children, such restraints, burdens and limitations, as, in its mature judgment, it deemed wise, right and proper.

But, your fathers, who had not adopted the fashionable idea of this day, of the infallibility of government, and the absolute character of its acts, presumed to differ from the home government in respect to the wisdom and the justice of some of those burdens and restraints. They went so far in their excitement as to pronounce the measures of government unjust, unreasonable, and oppressive, and altogether such as ought not to be quietly submitted to. I scarcely need say, fellow-citizens, that my opinion of those measures fully accords with that of your fathers. Such a declaration of agreement on my part would not be worth much to anybody. It would, certainly, prove nothing, as to what part I might have taken, had I lived during the great controversy of 1776. To say now that America was right, and England wrong, is exceedingly easy. Everybody can say it; the dastard, not less than the noble brave, can flippantly discant on the tyranny of England towards the American Colonies. It is fashionable to do so; but there was a time when to pronounce against England, and in favor of the cause of the colonies, tried men's souls. They who did so were accounted in their day, plotters of mischief, agitators and rebels, dangerous men. To side with the right, against the wrong, with the weak against the strong, and with the oppressed against the oppressor! here lies the merit, and the one which, of all others, seems unfashionable in our day. The cause of liberty may be stabbed by the men who glory in the deeds of your fathers. But, to proceed…

Conclusion

I have detained my audience entirely too long already. At some future period I will gladly avail myself of an opportunity to give this subject a full and fair discussion.

Allow me to say, in conclusion, notwithstanding the dark picture I have this day presented of the state of the nation, I do not despair of this country. There are forces in operation, which must inevitably work the downfall of slavery. "The arm of the Lord is not shortened," and the doom of slavery is certain. I, therefore, leave off where I began, with hope.

While drawing encouragement from the Declaration of Independence, the great principles it contains, and the genius of American Institutions, my spirit is also cheered by the obvious tendencies of the age. Nations do not now stand in the same relation to each other that they did ages ago. No nation can now shut itself up from the surrounding world, and trot round in the same old path of its fathers without interference. The time was when such could be done. Long established customs of hurtful character could formerly fence themselves in, and do their evil work with social impunity. Knowledge was then confined and enjoyed by the privileged few, and the multitude walked on in mental darkness. But a change has now come over the affairs of mankind. Walled cities and empires have become unfashionable. The arm of commerce has borne away the gates of the strong city. Intelligence is penetrating the darkest corners of the globe.

It makes its pathway over and under the sea, as well as on the earth. Wind, steam, and lightning are its chartered agents. Oceans no longer divide, but link nations together. From Boston to London is now a holiday excursion. Space is comparatively annihilated. Thoughts expressed on one side of the Atlantic, are distinctly heard on the other. The far off and almost fabulous Pacific rolls in grandeur at our feet. The Celestial Empire, the mystery of ages, is being solved. The fiat of the Almighty, "Let there be Light," has not yet spent its force. No abuse, no outrage whether in taste, sport or avarice, can now hide itself from the all-pervading light. The iron shoe, and crippled foot of China must be seen, in contrast with nature. Africa must rise and put on her yet unwoven garment. "Ethiopia shall stretch out her hand unto God." In the fervent aspirations of William Lloyd Garrison, I say, and let every heart join in saying it:

God speed the year of jubilee

The wide world o'er

When from their galling chains set free,

Th' oppress'd shall vilely bend the knee,

And wear the yoke of tyranny

Like brutes no more.

That year will come, and freedom's reign,

To man his plundered fights again

Restore.

God speed the day when human blood

Shall cease to flow!

In every clime be understood,

The claims of human brotherhood,

And each return for evil, good,

Not blow for blow;

That day will come all feuds to end.

And change into a faithful friend

Each foe.

God speed the hour, the glorious hour,

When none on earth

Shall exercise a lordly power,

Nor in a tyrant's presence cower;

But all to manhood's stature tower,

By equal birth!

That hour will come, to each, to all,

And from his prison-house, the thrall

Go forth.

Until that year, day, hour, arrive,

With head, and heart, and hand I'll strive,

To break the rod, and rend the gyve,

The spoiler of his prey deprive —

So witness Heaven!

And never from my chosen post,

Whate'er the peril or the cost,

Be driven.

Rhetorical Analysis / **What to the Slave...**

Instructions: In the space provided, answer the following questions concerning the purpose, audience, and tone of the speech to help you identify rhetorical appeals. Answer in complete sentences.

Criteria	Description

The Purpose of the Speech

Why did the orator deliver this speech? What was his goal?

The Audience of the Speech

Who was the audience? What was the occasion?

The Tone of the Speech

Tone is the way that an orator or an author feels about his work and the subject at hand.

How does the speaker feel about the subject he is speaking about?

Rhetorical Analysis / What to the Slave...

Instructions: Read over the quotations below from the speech, each of which makes an *appeal to ethos*. Then, explain how the reputation or the background of the speaker might have some bearing on how persuasive their speech might be. How does it help prove or support the speaker's argument?

Quotation	Description
Mr. President, Friends and Fellow Citizens: He who could address this audience without a quailing sensation, has stronger nerves than I have. I do not remember ever to have appeared as a speaker before any assembly more shrinkingly, nor with greater distrust of my ability, than I do this day.	
The fact is, ladies and gentlemen, the distance between this platform and the slave plantation, from which I escaped, is considerable — and the difficulties to be overcome in getting from the latter to the former, are by no means slight. That I am here to-day is, to me, a matter of astonishment as well as of gratitude.	
Fellow-citizens, I shall not presume to dwell at length on the associations that cluster about this day. The simple story of it is that, 76 years ago, the people of this country were British subjects. The style and title of your "sovereign people" (in which you now glory) was not then born. You were under the British Crown. Your fathers esteemed the English Government as the home government; and England as the fatherland.	

As far as appeals to ethos, why did Frederick Douglass seem to repeat the words fellow citizen?

....

....

....

....

....

....

As far as appeals to ethos, why did Douglass spend so much time recounting the early history of the founding of the United States?

....

....

....

....

....

....

The Canon of Memoria / What to the Slave...

Of the five canons, the canon of *memoria* may be the hardest canon to master. The practice of memorizing a speech requires considerable time and effort, but, like any skill, memorizing a speech becomes easier and easier the more things you try to memorize. We can use select speeches (like the one we just read) to practice our ability to memorize important passages and learn one method by which we can begin to memorize longer blocks of text. That method is to memorize one clause or sentence at a time, and then to go back and repeat *all of the sentences* you've memorized until you can recite the entire passage from memory.

> *Allow me to say, in conclusion, notwithstanding the dark picture I have this day presented of the state of the nation, I do not despair of this country. There are forces in operation, which must inevitably work the downfall of slavery. "The arm of the Lord is not shortened," and the doom of slavery is certain. I, therefore, leave off where I began, with hope. While drawing encouragement from the Declaration of Independence, the great principles it contains, and the genius of American Institutions, my spirit is also cheered by the obvious tendencies of the age.*

Step and Description	Lines from Speech
Step 1: Read the first clause or sentence out loud upwards of five to ten times. Try to recite the sentence without looking at the words.	*Allow me to say, in conclusion...*
Step 2: Read the next clause or sentence out loud upwards of five to ten times. Try to recite the sentence without looking at the words.	*...notwithstanding the dark picture I have this day...*
Step 3: Go back to the beginning and repeat the first two clauses or sentences. Repeat until you have memorized the passage in question.	*Allow me to say, in conclusion, notwithstanding the dark picture I have this day...*
Suggested Assignment: Recite the speech from memory for a homework, classwork, or assessment grade with one point for each word memorized (may also be taken as a percentage).	_____ /96 points

ESSAY

Writing Prompt

In the space provided, what was the most valuable concept or idea you learned about in this chapter? Why *that* idea or concept, and not another? If you have had opportunities to speak in public before, how might have the material in this chapter helped you? Reflect, too, on the speech(es) provided in this chapter: why did the ideas and goals communicated in the speech matter, and how did the speaker go about trying to persuade the audience to believe in them?

Appeal to Ethos / Nixon vs. Kennedy, 1960

NIXON VS. KENNEDY

Watch a video corresponding to this lesson:

https://bit.ly/3LIfpQE

Or, scan the QR Code below

Among the most famous presidential debates was that between candidates John F. Kennedy and Richard M. Nixon, held on September 26, 1960. The debate is famous for two reasons: one, the debate was the first to be broadcast live on television, and two, the debate revealed something extremely interesting about the *appeal to ethos*. When asked, people who watched the debate on television answered that Kennedy won the debate, but people who listened to the debate on the radio believed, instead, that Nixon won. So what happened, and what can we learn from this debate that would help us become better public speakers? Watch the video linked to the right and answer the questions below.

Question	Student Work
Who seems more relaxed? More confident?	
How does Kennedy come across on stage?	
How does Nixon look while Kennedy is speaking?	
And how does Nixon come across on stage?	
How does Kennedy look while Nixon is speaking?	
Why did people who watched the debate on television believe that Kennedy won?	
Why did people who listened to the debate on the radio believe that Nixon won?	

THE US CAPITOL / EAST SIDE
Photo by Martin Falbisoner

06

CHAPTER

Appeals to *Pathos*

ROADMAP

+ Review Aristotle's *Rhetoric* and the *Three Modes of Persuasion*.

+ Learn about appeals to *pathos* and how to frame an appeal to *ethos*.

+ Read selections from John F. Kennedy *We Will Go to the Moon* and Andrew Jackson's *Bank Veto Address*.

THALES
OUTCOME

№ 1

A person with **Unfailing Integrity**
Exemplifies integrity while developing trusting relationships.

An appeal to *pathos* is the appeal to the emotions. In the *Rhetoric*, Aristotle carefully distinguishes between *good* and the *bad* emotions based on the types of actions to which these emotions may give rise. An appeal to the emotions is one of the most powerful rhetorical appeals someone can make in a speech, and we must take every precaution that our appeals would not be *manipulative* or self-serving—such actions are not in line with Quintilian's *ideal orator*.

Appeals to Pathos

PATHOS COMES FROM the Greek word for *suffering* or *experience*. In short, an appeal to **pathos** is an appeal to the emotions. Aristotle, in the *Rhetoric*, states that "since rhetoric exists to affect the giving of decisions...he must also...put his hearers, who are to decide into the right frame of mind," (59). Emotional appeals present one of the most effective ways to help direct your hearers into the "right frame of mind." A speech that appeals to the emotional needs of your audience may appeal to their sense of pity, fear, jealousy, honor, or pride. Emotions may be the most powerful way to stir the wills of the men and women listening to your speech, and people are far more likely to do things their hearts want them to do than the course of action put forward by their heads. But, use such appeals wisely and responsibly—some of the worst and most vile orators in history used such appeals to the emotions. In the process, they brought ruin upon everyone who listened and accepted such arguments.

Aristotle devotes many pages in the *Rhetoric* to pathos and the myriad ways an orator can conduct such an appeal. Aristotle defines the "Emotions" as "those feelings that so change men as to affect their judgments, and that are also attended by pain or pleasure," (60). Aristotle obtained this definition, and the list of relevant emotions like "anger, pity, fear, and the like, with their opposites" by spending countless hours studying the speeches of noteworthy orators in the Athenian assembly (60).

We should again stress how one should never intentionally manipulate other individuals. That would be wrong and go against the spirit of Quintilian's *ideal orator*. History has countless examples of individuals

PLATO & ARISTOTLE
Raphael's School of Athens *(1509-1511)*

who used their rhetorical and public speaking skills to further their own agendas and manipulate people by making such appeals to the emotions. The Greeks even had a word for such leaders and speakers: **demagogue**. The word *demagogue* may sound like a monster from a fantasy novel—although in some ways, it is — but a demagogue is actually the name of a particular type of politician, one who uses their rhetorical skills solely

Vocabulary

Pathos

The appeal to the emotions.

Demagogue

From the Greek *demos* for "people" and *agogos* for "driver", a demagogue is a leader who uses his rhetorical and public speaking abilities to advance his own interests and not those of the broader community.

for their own power and influence. The word comes from the Greek *demos*, meaning "people" (as in *democracy*), and *agogos*, meaning "leader" or "driver". Thus, the name *demagogue* literally means a *driver* or a *leader of people*.

The word *demagogue* appeared first in ancient Athens to refer to a class of self-serving politicians. These politicians were willing to do or say just about anything to obtain political power. Athens was a democracy, so that political power ultimately resided in the people; the expression of that power was in a majority vote; and such a majority vote could be obtained by appealing to whatever the people wanted without much regard to what was best. At times, a demagogue might claim that the safety of the people was threatened by some outside power, and only they, the demagogues, could stop them.

Moreover, a demagogue could obtain political power by appealing to these emotions—fear, jealousy, and hatred. All people can feel these emotions at one time or another, and emotions are not necessarily bad in themselves (well, jealousy is…and so is enmity, too). But, if an individual were to indulge these emotions for too long, or begin to act on them, or to vote for policies born out of these emotions, it might spell ruin for those individuals, or the entire state, guided by these base, irrational instincts. Here are the words of Aristotle on one such politician, Cleon, from Aristotle's *Constitution of the Athenians*:

> *Then came Themistocles and Aristides, and after them Ephialtes as leader of the people, and Cimon son of Miltiades of the wealthier class. Pericles followed as leader of the people, and Thucydides, who was connected by marriage with Cimon, of the opposition.*
>
> *After the death of Pericles, Nicias, who subsequently fell in Sicily, appeared as leader of the aristocracy, and Cleon son of Cleaenetus of the people. The latter seems, more than any one else, to have been the cause of the corruption of the democracy by his wild undertakings; and he was the first to use unseemly shouting and coarse abuse on the Bema, and to harangue the people with his cloak girt up short about him, whereas all his predecessors had spoken decently and in order.*

As a result, we present this material in the spirit of helping you to discern truth from falsehood and to identify when an unscrupulous orator—individuals whom the ancients called demagogues—we have provided the same sort of close analysis of the bad emotions, too.

But appeals to *pathos* are not bad in and of themselves. The coach of a sports team, for example, should not use rational arguments to inspire his players to give it their all; instead, the coach should remind them of the pride, rightly understood, they would earn if they won. Aristotle might call that an appeal to the emotion of *confidence*. People are generally moved more by their emotions than by logical arguments, so if an orator wants to inspire the audience to take up a cause greater than themselves, then an emotional appeal would be one of the most effective means of doing so. In short, if the orator means to inspire the audience to *good* things, then an emotional appeal can be wholeheartedly proper and good, too. If an orator abuses emotional appeals, the fault is in the orator, not the kind of appeal being made.

To use emotional appeals in the right way, we should return to our first principles: Quintilian's idea of the *ideal orator*. That ideal orator is a public speaker who uses his rhetorical gifts to persuade the audience to not only *know* what is good but to *choose* what is good, too. As a result, orators should use emotional appeals when the occasion warrants it, perhaps in reminding people of the joy that comes with hard work, patriotism, and virtuous conduct. That is, they should make emotional appeals to persuade their audience to do or be better.

In line with good and bad appeals to *pathos*, Aristotle divides the emotions into two classes—one *good* and one *bad*. Those *good* emotions include *confidence* and

ARISTOTLE AND HIS PUPIL, ALEXANDER.

ARISTOTLE TEACHING ALEXANDER THE GREAT
Illustration by Charles Laplante (1866).

friendliness, and if an orator wants to persuade the audience to be good, then they might want to make appeals to these *good* emotions. Aristotle also pairs each *good* emotion with its corresponding *bad* emotion. For example, Aristotle cites *fear* as the opposite of *confidence*, and *enmity* as the opposite of *friendship*.

While Aristotle's idea of the emotions differs from our own modern understanding, we still want to go back to the sources and read Aristotle's own words for ourselves. To help with this task, we have provided the text from Aristotle's *Rhetoric* where he identifies each emotion and explains how that emotion operates, as well as blank space for you to paraphrase Aristotle's description in your own words.

Appeal to Pathos / The Good Emotions

Instructions: Aristotle divides emotions into *good* and *bad* emotions—*good* being an emotional state we should pursue and *bad* being such a state we should avoid. In the table below, read over the quotation from Aristotle's *Rhetoric*, then paraphrase Aristotle's definition in your own words.

The Emotion	Aristotle's Definition	Aristotle's Definition, Paraphrased in Your Own Words
Friendliness *Opposite of Enmity*	*We may describe friendly feeling towards any one as wishing for him what you believe to be good things, not for your own sake but for his, and being inclined, so far as you can, to bring these things about...things that cause friendship are: doing kindnesses; doing them unasked; and not proclaiming the fact when they are done, which shows that they are done for our own sake and for for some other reason,* (66-67, 68).	
Calm *Opposite of Anger*	Calm, *the opposite of* anger, *may be defined as settling down or quieting of anger.... we feel calm towards those who humble themselves before us and do not [deny or contradict] us... our anger ceases towards those who humble themselves before us ...we also feel calm towards those who are serious when we are serious ... also towards those who have done us more kindnesses than we have done them,* (64-65).	
Confidence *Opposite of Fear* **Editor's Note:** We should note the famous Aristotelian idea that *courage* is the midpoint between *foolhardiness* and *cowardice*.	Confidence *is the opposite of* fear, *and what causes it is the opposite of what causes fear; it is, therefore, the expectation associated with a mental picture of the nearness of what keeps us safe and the absence or remoteness of what is terrible...we feel confidence if we believe we have often succeeded and never suffered reverses, or have often met danger and escaped it safely,* (71).	

Appeal to Pathos / The Good Emotions

Instructions: Aristotle divides emotions into *good* and *bad* emotions—*good* being an emotional state we should pursue and *bad* being such a state we should avoid. In the table below, read over the quotation from Aristotle's *Rhetoric*, then paraphrase Aristotle's definition in your own words.

The Emotion	Aristotle's Definition	Aristotle's Definition, Paraphrased in Your Own Words
Emulation *Opposite of Envy*	As opposed to envy, *emulation is pain caused by seeing the presence, in person whose nature is like our own, of good things that are highly valued and are possible for ourselves to acquire; but it is felt not because others have these goods, but because we have not got them ourselves. It is therefore a good feeling felt by good persons, whereas envy is a bad feeling felt by bad persons*, (82-83).	
Kindness *Opposite of Meanness*	The influence of which a man is said to 'be kind' *may be defined as helpfulness towards some one in need, not in return for anything, nor for the advantage of the helper himself, but for that of the person helped. Kindness is great if shown to one who is in great need, or who needs what is important and hard to get, or who needs it at an important and difficult crisis; or if the helper is the only, the first, or the chief person to give the help*, (76).	
Pity *Opposite of Callousness*	*Pity may be defined as a feeling of pain caused by the sight of some evil, destructive or painful, which befalls one who does not deserve it, and which we might expect to befall ourselves or some friend of ours, and moreover to befall us soon*, (77).	

Appeal to Pathos / The Bad Emotions

Instructions: Aristotle divides emotions into *good* and *bad* emotions—*good* being an emotional state we should pursue and *bad* being such a state we should avoid. In the table below, read over the quotation from Aristotle's *Rhetoric*, then paraphrase Aristotle's definition in your own words.

The Emotion	Aristotle's Definition	Aristotle's Definition, Paraphrased in Your Own Words
Shame *Opposite of Shamelessness*	Shame may be *defined as pain or disturbance in regard to bad things, whether present, past, or future, which seem likely to involve us in discredit,* (72).	
Anger *Opposite of Calm*	*Anger may be defined as an impulse, accompanied by pain, to a conspicuous revenge for a conspicuous slight directed without justification towards what concerns oneself or towards what concern's one's friends. If this is a proper definition of anger, it must always be felt towards some particular individual, e.g. Cleon, and not 'man' in general. It must be felt because the other has done or intended to do something to him or one of his friends. It must always be attended by a certain pleasure—that which arises from the expectation of revenge,* (60).	
Fear *Opposite of Confidence*	*Fear may be defined as a pain or disturbance due to a mental picture of some destructive or painful evil in the future...such as amount to great pains or lesses And even these only if they appear not remote but so near as to be imminent,* (69).	

Appeal to Pathos / The Bad Emotions

Instructions: Aristotle divides emotions into *good* and *bad* emotions—*good* being an emotional state we should pursue and *bad* being such a state we should avoid. In the table below, read over the quotation from Aristotle's *Rhetoric*, then paraphrase Aristotle's definition in your own words.

The Emotion	Aristotle's Definition	Aristotle's Definition, Paraphrased in Your Own Words
Enmity & Hatred *Opposite of Friendliness*	*Enmity may be produced by anger or spite...now whereas anger arises from offenses against oneself, enmity may arise even without that; we may hate people merely because of what we take to be their character. Anger is always concerned with individuals...whereas hatred is directed also against classes,* (69).	
Unkindness *Opposite of Kindness*	Unkindness is the opposite of kindness, so that unkind people may *have been helpful simply to promote their own interest...their action was accidental, or was forced upon them; or that they were not doing a favor, but merely returning one,* (76).	
Envy *Opposite of Emulation*	*Envy is pain at the sight of such good fortune as consists of the good things already mentioned; we feel it towards our equals; not with the idea of getting something for ourselves, but because the other people have it....We feel envy also if we fall but a little short of having everything,* (81).	

Appeal to Pathos

Instructions: Read over the following examples of various appeals to the emotions. In the space provided, identify to what emotion the example appeals and whether it is an example of a *good* or *bad* emotion, as listed above.

Example: I know this action seems wrong but if you were my friend, you would do this favor for me.

This argument is an example of an appeal to *unkindness*, as the speaker says that someone should do this favor for them (whatever it is) based on their relationship. A real friend would never ask you to do something wrong.

1. We should volunteer at the local food pantry because the people who go to that food pantry are our neighbors, neighbors even if we do not know them.

2. We have to do whatever it takes to win against our crosstown rivals because they have humiliated us in past games.

3. The rich do not pay their fair share of taxes, so let's enact new tax policies that would ensure that they do.

4. If we do not stand up for ourselves and our rights now, we will be overrun by our enemies!

5. Let us imitate the example of such brave individuals, for they lived lives that are full of goodness, truth, and beauty.

Appeal to Pathos

Instructions: Read over the following examples of various appeals to the emotions. In the space provided, identify to what emotion the example appeals and whether it is an example of a *good* or *bad* emotion, as listed above.

6. Let's help out at the next student council dance since, well, the student council helped us out with our last big project.

7. Let's calm down and think before we make any decisions, knowing how easily things can go wrong if we act rashly.

8. We should be happy when others succeed because it reminds us that we, too, are capable of great things.

9. We should be upset when others succeed because we are not getting the praise, honor, and rewards we deserve.

10. Let's try our best, knowing that if we win, we'll have bragging rights over our cross-town rivals!

Rhetorical Analysis / Jackson's Bank Veto

Instructions: Identify appeals to pathos in two famous speeches from American history. The first is Andrew Jackson's Bank Veto of 1832. The second is John F. Kennedy's Address at Rice University on September 12, 1962.

Andrew Jackson was born in 1767 somewhere near the border between North and South Carolina. Jackson eventually migrated to Tennessee and made a reputation for himself as a frontier lawyer and soldier, quickly rising through the ranks of Tennessee's political scene. Jackson's political future was set when he won a shocking upset against the British in the Battle of New Orleans during the War of 1812. Jackson was elected to the U.S. House of Representative and the U.S. Senate, and was eventually elected president in 1829. After his reelection in 1832, Jackson moved to revoke the charter for the Bank of the United States, an institution Jackson believed encouraged political corruption, unwise financial programs, and hindered the social and material progress of ordinary Americans. So, on July 10, 1832, Jackson delivered the following address just as he vetoed this bill. The following excerpt is from the conclusion of Andrew Jackson's address on the Bank Veto, delivered to the U.S. Senate on July 10, 1832.

July 10, 1832

Under such circumstances the bank comes forward and asks a renewal of its charter for a term of fifteen years upon conditions which not only operate as a gratuity to the stockholders of many millions of dollars, but will sanction any abuses and legalize any encroachments.

Suspicions are entertained and charges are made of gross abuse and violation of its charter. An investigation unwillingly conceded and so restricted in time as necessarily to make it incomplete and unsatisfactory discloses enough to excite suspicion and alarm. In the practices of the principal bank partially unveiled, in the absence of important witnesses, and in numerous charges confidently made and as yet wholly uninvestigated there was enough to induce a majority of the committee of investigation-a committee which was selected from the most able and honorable members of the House of Representatives-to recommend a suspension of further action upon the bill and a prosecution of the inquiry. As the charter had yet four years to run, and as a renewal now was not necessary to the successful prosecution of its business, it was to have been expected that the bank itself, conscious of its purity and proud of its character, would have withdrawn its application for the present, and demanded the severest scrutiny into all its transactions. In their declining to do so there seems to be an additional reason why the functionaries of the Government should proceed with less haste and more caution in the [renewal] of their monopoly.

The bank is professedly established as an agent of the executive branch of the Government, and its constitutionality is maintained on that ground. Neither upon the propriety of present action nor upon the provisions of this act was the Executive consulted. It has had no opportunity to say that it neither needs nor wants an agent clothed with such powers and favored by such exemptions. There is nothing in its legitimate functions which makes it necessary or proper. Whatever interest or influence, whether public or private, has given birth to this act, it can not be found either in the wishes or necessities of the executive department, by which present action is deemed premature, and the powers conferred upon its agent not only unnecessary, but dangerous to the Government and country.

It is to be regretted that the rich and powerful too often bend the acts of government to their selfish purposes. Distinctions in society will always exist under every just government. Equality of talents, of education, or of wealth can not be produced by human institutions. In the full enjoyment of the gifts of Heaven and the fruits of superior industry, economy, and virtue, every man is equally entitled to protection by law; but when the laws undertake to add to these natural and just advantages artificial distinctions, to grant titles, gratuities, and exclusive privileges, to make the rich richer and the potent more powerful, the humble members of society-the farmers, mechanics, and laborers-who have neither the time nor the means of securing like favors to themselves, have a right to complain of the injustice of their Government. There are no necessary evils in government. Its evils exist only in its abuses. If it would confine itself to equal protection, and, as Heaven does its rains, shower its favors alike on the high and the low, the rich and the poor, it would be an unqualified blessing. In the act before me there seems to be a wide and unnecessary departure from these just principles.

Nor is our Government to be maintained or our Union preserved by invasions of the rights and powers of the several States. In thus attempting to make our General Government strong we make it weak. Its true strength consists in leaving individuals and States as much as possible to themselves-in making itself felt, not in its power, but in its beneficence; not in its control, but in its protection; not in binding the States more closely to the center, but leaving each to move unobstructed in its proper orbit.

Experience should teach us wisdom. Most of the difficulties our Government now encounters and most of the dangers which impend over our Union have sprung from an abandonment of the legitimate objects of Government by our national legislation, and the adoption of such principles as are embodied in this act. Many of our rich men have not been content with equal protection and equal benefits, but have besought us to make them richer by act of Congress. By attempting to gratify their desires we have in the results of our legislation arrayed section against section, interest against interest, and man against man, in a fearful commotion which threatens to shake the foundations of our Union. It is time to pause in our career to review our principles, and if possible revive that devoted patriotism and spirit of compromise which distinguished the sages of the Revolution and the fathers of our Union. If we cannot at once, in justice to interests vested under improvident legislation, make our Government what it ought to be, we can at least take a stand against all new grants of monopolies and exclusive privileges, against any prostitution of our Government to the advancement of the few at the expense of the many, and in favor of compromise and gradual reform in our code of laws and system of political economy.

I have now done my duty to my country. If sustained by my fellow citizens, I shall be grateful and happy; if not, I shall find in the motives which impel me ample grounds for contentment and peace. In the difficulties which surround us and the dangers which threaten our institutions there is cause for neither dismay nor alarm. For relief and deliverance let us firmly rely on that kind Providence which I am sure watches with peculiar care over the destinies of our Republic, and on the intelligence and wisdom of our countrymen. Through His abundant goodness and heir patriotic devotion our liberty and Union will be preserved.

Rhetorical Analysis / Jackson's Bank Veto

Instructions: In the space provided, answer the following questions concerning the purpose, audience, and tone of the speech to help you identify the kind of rhetorical appeals used in the speech. Answer in complete sentences.

Criteria	Description
## The Purpose of the Speech *Why did the orator deliver this speech? What was his goal?*	
## The Audience of the Speech *Who was the audience? What was the occasion?*	
## The Tone of the Speech *Tone is the way that an orator or an author feels about his work and the subject at hand.* *How does the speaker feel about the subject he is speaking about?*	

Rhetorical Analysis / **Jackson's Bank Veto**

Instructions: Each of the quotations below makes an *appeal to pathos*. In the space provided, explain the nature of the appeal, the emotion the speaker appeals to (see Aristotle's explanation of *good* and *bad* emotions), and how the appeal serves to make the speech more persuasive, if at all. How does it help prove or support the speaker's argument?

Quotation	Description
Suspicions are entertained and charges are made of gross abuse and violation of its charter. An investigation unwillingly conceded and so restricted in time as necessarily to make it incomplete and unsatisfactory discloses enough to excite suspicion and alarm.	
In their declining to do so there seems to be an additional reason why the functionaries of the Government should proceed with less haste and more caution in the [renewal] of their monopoly.	
Whatever interest or influence, whether public or private, has given birth to this act, it can not be found either in the wishes or necessities of the executive department, by which present action is deemed premature, and the powers conferred upon its agent not only unnecessary, but dangerous to the Government and country.	
Nor is our Government to be maintained or our Union preserved by invasions of the rights and powers of the several States. In thus attempting to make our General Government strong we make it weak. Its true strength consists in leaving individuals and States as much as possible to themselves-in making itself felt, not in its power, but in its beneficence; not in its control, but in its protection; not in binding the States more closely to the center, but leaving each to move unobstructed in its proper orbit.	

Rhetorical Analysis / We Go to the Moon

Instructions: As with the previous speech, identify the various appeals to *pathos* in John F. Kennedy's Address at Rice University on September 12, 1962, sometimes titled *We Go to the Moon*.

John F. Kennedy was born into a prosperous New England family in 1917. His father, Joseph Kennedy, was a banker and stock broker, making a fortune before the market crash of 1929. Kennedy would attend Harvard and enlisted in the Navy during World War II, serving in the Pacific Theater. After the war, Kennedy was elected to the U.S. House of Representatives, the U.S. Senate, and the office of the President in 1960. Kennedy's popularity rested on a unique combination of charisma, his father's considerable wealth used to finance Kennedy's early campaigns, and Kennedy's own noteworthy public speaking abilities. Kennedy's speeches contain stirring appeals to *pathos*, appeals that lead the listener to believe that practically anything is possible.

September 12, 1962

President Pitzer, Mr. Vice President, Governor, Congressman Thomas, Senator Wiley, and Congressman Miller, Mr. Webb, Mr. Bell, scientists, distinguished guests, and ladies and gentlemen:

I appreciate your president having made me an honorary visiting professor, and I will assure you that my first lecture will be very brief.

I am delighted to be here, and I'm particularly delighted to be here on this occasion.

We meet at a college noted for knowledge, in a city noted for progress, in a State noted for strength, and we stand in need of all three, for we meet in an hour of change and challenge, in a decade of hope and fear, in an age of both knowledge and ignorance. The greater our knowledge increases, the greater our ignorance unfolds.

Despite the striking fact that most of the scientists that the world has ever known are alive and working today, despite the fact that this Nation's own scientific manpower is doubling every 12 years in a rate of growth more than three times that of our population as a whole, despite that, the vast stretches of the unknown and the unanswered and the unfinished still far outstrip our collective comprehension.

No man can fully grasp how far and how fast we have come, but condense, if you will, the 50,000 years of man's recorded history in a time span of but a half-century. Stated in these terms, we know very little about the first 40 years, except at the end of them advanced man had learned to use the skins of animals to cover them. Then about 10 years ago, under this standard, man emerged from his caves to construct other kinds of shelter. Only five years ago man learned to write and use a cart with wheels. Christianity began less than two years ago.

The printing press came this year, and then less than two months ago, during this whole 50-year span of human history, the steam engine provided a new source of power.

Newton explored the meaning of gravity. Last month electric lights and telephones and automobiles and airplanes became available. Only last week did we develop penicillin and television and nuclear power, and now if America's new spacecraft succeeds in reaching Venus, we will have literally reached the stars before midnight tonight.

This is a breathtaking pace, and such a pace cannot help but create new ills as it dispels old, new ignorance, new problems, new dangers. Surely the opening vistas of space promise high costs and hardships, as well as high reward.

So it is not surprising that some would have us stay where we are a little longer to rest, to wait. But this city of Houston, this State of Texas, this country of the United States was not built by those who waited and rested and wished to look behind them. This country was conquered by those who moved forward—and so will space.

William Bradford, speaking in 1630 of the founding of the Plymouth Bay Colony, said that all great and honorable actions are accompanied with great difficulties, and both must be enterprised and overcome with answerable courage.

If this capsule history of our progress teaches us anything, it is that man, in his quest for knowledge and progress, is determined and cannot be deterred. The exploration of space will go ahead, whether we join in it or not, and it is one of the great adventures of all time, and no nation which expects to be the leader of other nations can expect to stay behind in the race for space.

Those who came before us made certain that this country rode the first waves of the industrial revolutions, the first waves of modern invention, and the first wave of nuclear power, and this generation does not intend to founder in the backwash of the coming age of space. We mean to be a part of it—we mean to lead it. For the eyes of the world now look into space, to the moon and to the planets beyond, and we have vowed that we shall not see it governed by a hostile flag of conquest, but by a banner of freedom and peace. We have vowed that we shall not see space filled with weapons of mass destruction, but with instruments of knowledge and understanding.

Yet the vows of this Nation can only be fulfilled if we in this Nation are first, and, therefore, we intend to be first. In short, our leadership in science and in industry, our hopes for peace and security, our obligations to ourselves as well as others, all require us to make this effort, to solve these mysteries, to solve them for the good of all men, and to become the world's leading space-faring nation.

We set sail on this new sea because there is new knowledge to be gained, and new rights to be won, and they must be won and used for the progress of all people. For space science, like nuclear science and all technology, has no conscience of its own. Whether it will become a force for good or ill depends on man, and only if the United States occupies a position of pre-eminence can we help decide whether this new ocean will be a sea of peace or a new terrifying theater of war. I do not say that we should or will go unprotected against the hostile misuse of space any more than we go unprotected against the hostile use of land or sea, but I do say that space can be explored and mastered without feeding the fires of war, without repeating the mistakes that man has made in extending his writ around this globe of ours.

There is no strife, no prejudice, no national conflict in outer space as yet. Its hazards are hostile to us all. Its conquest deserves the best of all mankind, and its opportunity for peaceful cooperation many never come again. But why, some say, the moon? Why choose this as our goal? And they may ask why climb the highest mountain? Why, 35 years ago, fly the Atlantic? Why does Rice play Texas?

We choose to go to the moon. We choose to go to the moon in this decade and do the other things, not because they are easy, but because they are hard, because that goal will serve to organize and measure the best of our energies and skills, because that challenge is one that we are willing to accept, one we are unwilling to postpone, and one which we intend to win, and the others, too.

It is for these reasons that I regard the decision last year to shift our efforts in space from low to high gear as among the most important decisions that will be made during my incumbency in the office of the Presidency.

In the last 24 hours we have seen facilities now being created for the greatest and most complex exploration in man's history. We have felt the ground shake and the air shattered by the testing of a Saturn C-1 booster rocket, many times as powerful as the Atlas which launched John Glenn, generating power equivalent to 10,000 automobiles with their accelerators on the floor. We have seen the site where the F-1 rocket engines, each one as powerful as all eight engines of the Saturn combined, will be clustered together to make the advanced Saturn missile, assembled in a new building to be built at Cape Canaveral as tall as a 48 story structure, as wide as a city block, and as long as two lengths of this field.

Within these last 19 months at least 45 satellites have circled the earth. Some 40 of them were "made in the United States of America" and they were far more sophisticated and supplied far more knowledge to the people of the world than those of the Soviet Union.

The Mariner spacecraft now on its way to Venus is the most intricate instrument in the history of space science. The accuracy of that shot is comparable to firing a missile from Cape Canaveral and dropping it in this stadium between the 40-yard lines.

Transit satellites are helping our ships at sea to steer a safer course. Tiros satellites have given us unprecedented warnings of hurricanes and storms, and will do the same for forest fires and icebergs.

We have had our failures, but so have others, even if they do not admit them. And they may be less public.

To be sure, we are behind, and will be behind for some time in manned flight. But we do not intend to stay behind, and in this decade, we shall make up and move ahead.

The growth of our science and education will be enriched by new knowledge of our universe and environment, by new techniques of learning and mapping and observation, by new tools and computers for industry, medicine, the home as well as the school. Technical institutions, such as Rice, will reap the harvest of these gains.

And finally, the space effort itself, while still in its infancy, has already created a great number of new companies, and tens of thousands of new jobs. Space and related industries are generating new demands in investment and skilled personnel, and this city and this State, and this region, will share greatly in this growth. What was once the furthest outpost on the old frontier of the West will be the furthest outpost on the new frontier of science and space. Houston, your City of Houston, with its Manned Spacecraft Center, will become the heart of a large scientific and engineering community. During the next 5 years the National Aeronautics and Space Administration expects to double the number of scientists and engineers in this area, to increase its outlays for salaries and expenses to $60 million a year; to invest some $200 million in plant and laboratory facilities; and to direct or contract for new space efforts over $1 billion from this Center in this City.

To be sure, all this costs us all a good deal of money. This year's space budget is three times what it was in January 1961, and it is greater than the space budget of the previous eight years combined. That budget now stands at $5,400 million a year—a staggering sum, though somewhat less than we pay for cigarettes and cigars every year. Space expenditures will soon rise some more, from 40 cents per person per week to more than 50 cents a week for every man, woman and child in the United States, for we have given this program a high national priority—even though I realize that this is in some measure an act of faith and vision, for we do not now know what benefits await us.

But if I were to say, my fellow citizens, that we shall send to the moon, 240,000 miles away from the control station in Houston, a giant rocket more than 300 feet tall, the length of this football field, made of new metal alloys, some of which have not yet been invented, capable of standing heat and stresses several times more than have ever been experienced, fitted together with a precision better than the finest watch, carrying all the equipment needed for propulsion, guidance, control, communications, food and survival, on an untried mission, to an unknown celestial body, and then return it safely to earth, re-entering the atmosphere at speeds of over 25,000 miles per hour, causing heat about half that of the temperature of the sun—almost as hot as it is here today—and do all this, and do it right, and do it first before this decade is out—then we must be bold.

I'm the one who is doing all the work, so we just want you to stay cool for a minute. [*laughter from audience*]

However, I think we're going to do it, and I think that we must pay what needs to be paid. I don't think we ought to waste any money, but I think we ought to do the job. And this will be done in the decade of the sixties. It may be done while some of you are still here at school at this college and university. It will be done during the term of office of some of the people who sit here on this platform. But it will be done. And it will be done before the end of this decade.

I am delighted that this university is playing a part in putting a man on the moon as part of a great national effort of the United States of America.

Many years ago the great British explorer George Mallory, who was to die on Mount Everest, was asked why did he want to climb it. He said, "Because it is there."

Well, space is there, and we're going to climb it, and the moon and the planets are there, and new hopes for knowledge and peace are there. And, therefore, as we set sail we ask God's blessing on the most hazardous and dangerous and greatest adventure on which man has ever embarked.

Thank you.

Rhetorical Analysis / We Go to the Moon

Instructions: In the space provided, answer the following questions concerning the purpose, audience, and tone of the speech to help you identify the kind of rhetorical appeals used in the speech. Answer in complete sentences.

Criteria	Description
## The Purpose of the Speech *Why did the orator deliver this speech? What was his goal?*	
## The Audience of the Speech *Who was the audience? What was the occasion?*	
## The Tone of the Speech *Tone is the way that an orator or an author feels about his work and the subject at hand.* *How does the speaker feel about the subject he is speaking about?*	

ACTIVITY

Rhetorical Analysis / **We Go to the Moon**

Instructions: Each of the quotations below makes an *appeal to pathos*. In the space provided, explain the nature of the appeal, the emotion the speaker appeals to (see Aristotle's explanation of *good* and *bad* emotions), and how the appeal serves to make the speech more persuasive, if at all. How does it help prove or support the speaker's argument?

Quotation	Description
We meet at a college noted for knowledge, in a city noted for progress, in a State noted for strength, and we stand in need of all three, for we meet in an hour of change and challenge, in a decade of hope and fear, in an age of both knowledge and ignorance. The greater our knowledge increases, the greater our ignorance unfolds.	
For the eyes of the world now look into space, to the moon and to the planets beyond, and we have vowed that we shall not see it governed by a hostile flag of conquest, but by a banner of freedom and peace. We have vowed that we shall not see space filled with weapons of mass destruction, but with instruments of knowledge and understanding.	
In short, our leadership in science and in industry, our hopes for peace and security, our obligations to ourselves as well as others, all require us to make this effort, to solve these mysteries, to solve them for the good of all men, and to become the world's leading space-faring nation.	
We choose to go to the moon. We choose to go to the moon in this decade and do the other things, not because they are easy, but because they are hard, because that goal will serve to organize and measure the best of our energies and skills, because that challenge is one that we are willing to accept, one we are unwilling to postpone, and one which we intend to win, and the others, too.	

As far as appeals to pathos, did Andrew Jackson appeal to more of the bad or more of the good emotions? If he seemed to favor one set of emotions over the other, why do you think he made this choice?

....

....

....

....

....

....

As far as appeals to pathos, did John F. Kennedy appeal to more of the bad or more of the good emotions? If he seemed to favor one set of emotions over the other, why do you think he made this choice?

....

....

....

....

....

....

Canon of Memory / We Go to the Moon

Of the five canons, the canon of *memoria* may be the hardest canon to master. The practice of memorizing a speech requires considerable time and effort, but, like any skill, memorizing a speech becomes easier and easier the more things you try to memorize. We can use select speeches (like the one we just read) to practice our ability to memorize important passages and learn one method by which we can begin to memorize longer blocks of text. That method is to memorize one clause or sentence at a time, and then to go back and repeat *all of the sentences* you've memorized until you can recite the entire passage from memory.

> *We choose to go to the moon. We choose to go to the moon in this decade and do the other things, not because they are easy, but because they are hard, because that goal will serve to organize and measure the best of our energies and skills, because that challenge is one that we are willing to accept, one we are unwilling to postpone, and one which we intend to win, and the others, too.*

Step and Description	Lines from Speech
Step 1: Read the first clause or sentence out loud upwards of five to ten times. Try to recite the sentence without looking at the words.	*We choose to go to the moon...*
Step 2: Read the next clause or sentence out loud upwards of five to ten times. Try to recite the sentence without looking at the words.	*We choose to go to the moon in this decade and do the other things ...*
Step 3: Go back to the beginning and repeat the first two clauses or sentences. Repeat until you have memorized the passage in question.	*We choose to go to the moon. We choose to go to the moon in this decade and do the other things ...*
Suggested Assignment: Recite the speech from memory for a homework, classwork, or assessment grade with one point for each word memorized (may also be taken as a percentage).	_____ / 76 points

Writing Prompt

In the space provided, what was the most valuable concept or idea you learned about in this chapter? Why *that* idea or concept, and not another? If you have had opportunities to speak in public before, how might have the material in this chapter helped you? Reflect, too, on the speech(es) provided in this chapter: why did the ideas and goals communicated in the speech matter, and how did the speaker go about trying to persuade the audience to believe in them?

The Kinds of Speeches

ROADMAP

✦ Learn about the different kinds of speeches and how each kind of speech is well-suited to one particular occasion.

✦ Learn about panegyric, forensic or judicial oratory, and deliberative oratory.

✦ Read selections from the speeches of John Adams, Martin Luther King, Jr., and Abraham Lincoln.

THALES OUTCOME

Nº 2

A Virtuous Leader with Well-Developed Judgment *combines thinking skills and traits such as humility, generosity, and courage..*

Leaders are often called upon to deliver speeches at moments of great importance or times of crisis. Their ability to craft a speech that speaks to the issues at hand and helps their audience understand the significance of those events is an indispensable component of virtuous leadership, a component we hope to demonstrate through the three noteworthy speeches we have selected in this chapter.

The Kinds of Oratory

ANCIENT RHETORICIANS DIVIDED rhetoric into three kinds, differentiated by their purpose and setting. The first kind was **judicial** oratory, the kind of oratory used in law courts. The second was **deliberative** oratory, the kind that focuses on some future course of action. The third and last kind of oratory was called **panegyric**, which was used at solemn state occasions such as funerals or public ceremonies. Aristotle states that of the three elements that make up a speech, namely the audience, the speaker, and the subject, it is the audience who truly determines what kind of speech should be given. That is, the audience expects the orator to focus on certain things if the orator is speaking at a funeral versus in an assembly. Let's examine the three kinds of oratory now, beginning with *judicial* oratory.

Judicial Oratory

The first kind of oratory is judicial oratory, so named because it is used in the courtroom. Judicial oratory is also called *forensic* or *legal* oratory, and it is the type of speech one would expect to hear from a lawyer defending their client or the interests of the state. Chronologically, judicial oratory focused on events in the past, such as whether or not a crime had taken place and whether or not their client had committed the crime. Judicial oratory focused on thematic issues such as justice and injustice, the questions of innocence and guilt, and the weighing of evidence and testimony.

Orators relied on logical arguments and at times emotional appeals to support their client's cause—anything that could possibly move the hearts of the judge and the jury. Cicero, through the mouthpiece of Sulpicious in *On the Orator*, notes that should an orator recognize that an appeal to the emotions may be effective, the "feelings on which we have to work in the minds of the judges, or whoever they may be before whom we may plead, are love, hatred, anger, envy, pity, hope, joy, fear, anxiety," (Cicero 142; Aristotle 13; Corbett 39).

Deliberative Oratory

The second kind of speech is deliberative oratory, a kind of oratory that focused on identifying the correct course of action and arguing in support of it. This kind of rhetoric is most appropriate for a setting like the Roman Senate or in a council of generals on the battlefield, for the orator must know what is the best course of action and the best means of arguing to take

The three types of oratory include judicial oratory, deliberative oratory, and panegyric oratory; the orator knows what kind of argument he has to give based on the setting, the occasion, and the expectations of the audience.

Vocabulary

Write down this vocabulary in your notebook. These terms will help you better learn and understand the material in this chapter.

Judicial (or Forensic) Oratory

The kind of oratory used in law courts, aimed at persuading a judge or a jury.

Deliberative Oratory

The kind of oratory used in any kind of assembly where some future course of action is debated.

Panegyric Oratory

The kind of oratory used at solemn state occasions.

PERICLES / 495-429 BC
Athenian general and noted orator

whatever that course may be. Deliberative rhetoric may also be called *political*, *hortative* (*hortative* means "encouraging"), and *advisory* rhetoric. Deliberative rhetoric is appropriate for any setting where individuals are debating what they should do next. Chronologically, deliberative rhetoric focuses on the future and what ought to be, and thus deliberative speeches might contain both logical and emotional appeals. Deliberative rhetoric also tends to be more pragmatic and straightforward, thematically focused on what ought to be done and what is *expedient* or *inexpedient* (Corbett 39).

Panegyric Oratory

The last kind of rhetoric is panegyric oratory, a brand of oratory used on occasions like funerals and public ceremonies. At such formal occasions, the speaker would praise or criticize someone or some institution. This kind of oratory was also called *demonstrative, declamatory, epideictic,* and *ceremonial* oratory, as it was the kind of speech a politician might deliver at a state funeral, an inauguration, or some other great public ceremony. Aristotle says that such ceremonial oratory is focused on "either prais[ing] or censur[ing] somebody", and that chronologically, panegyric oratory is "concerned with the present, though they often find it useful also to recall the past and to make guesses about the future". He continues that the goal of an orator giving such a speech is to prove the individual being honored "worthy of [that] honour or the reverse, and they too treat all other considerations with reference to this one". As a result, panegyric speeches might contain more emotional appeals than rational ones (Aristotle 13; Corbett 39).

Kinds of Oratory / Guided Notes

In the space provided, answer the following questions about the *kinds of oratory* and what each kind of oratory focused on. Several blanks have already been filled to give you an idea of how you should fill in the rest of the chart.

The Kind of Oratory	Occasion	Chronological Focus	Thematic Aim / Focus	Appeals
Judicial (or Forensic) Oratory	A courtroom			
Deliberative Oratory		The future		
Panegyric Oratory			Praise or blame	

Rhetorical Analysis / The Gettysburg Address

Instructions: As with previous chapters, we have provided one noteworthy speech from American history. In this section, we have provided one speech as an example of *judicial oratory, deliberative oratory,* and *panegyric oratory,* but we have not provided any other information that may help you determine what kind of speech it is. Instead, read over the material covered in this chapter, identify what the speech focuses on, the appeals the speaker makes, and other relevant criteria.

On November 9, 1863, Lincoln and a host of Union politicians, generals, and notables gathered in Gettysburg, Pennsylvania, to dedicate the Soldiers' National Cemetery. As Lincoln himself states, the great battle of Gettysburg had taken place at this location four months earlier, in July 1-3, 1863, and they had gathered to honor the sacrifices of so many Union soldiers for the "new birth of freedom" Lincoln hoped the country would experience once the war had ended.

‖ ABRAHAM LINCOLN / 1809 - 1865

November 19, 1863

Four score and seven years ago our fathers brought forth on this continent, a new nation, conceived in Liberty, and dedicated to the proposition that all men are created equal.

Now we are engaged in a great civil war, testing whether that nation, or any nation so conceived and so dedicated, can long endure. We are met on a great battle-field of that war. We have come to dedicate a portion of that field, as a final resting place for those who here gave their lives that that nation might live. It is altogether fitting and proper that we should do this.

But, in a larger sense, we can not dedicate—we can not consecrate—we can not hallow—this ground. The brave men, living and dead, who struggled here, have consecrated it, far above our poor power to add or detract. The world will little note, nor long remember what we say here, but it can never forget what they did here. It is for us the living, rather, to be dedicated here to the unfinished work which they who fought here have thus far so nobly advanced. It is rather for us to be here dedicated to the great task remaining before us—that from these honored dead we take increased devotion to that cause for which they gave the last full measure of devotion—that we here highly resolve that these dead shall not have died in vain—that this nation, under God, shall have a new birth of freedom—and that government of the people, by the people, for the people, shall not perish from the earth.

Kinds of Oratory / **Guided Notes**

In the space provided, explain the *Occasion, the Chronological Focus, the Thematic Aim / Focus,* and the *Appeals* made in the previous speech.

Element	Student Work
Occasion	
Chronological Focus	
Thematic Aim / Focus	
Appeals	

Rhetorical Analysis / Address to the Jury

Instructions: Our second speech comes from John Adams, the second president of the United States. John Adams was born in Braintree, Massachusetts, received a traditional, classical education, and eventually matriculated to Harvard, one of only a few colleges in the American colonies. Before Adams became one of the most outspoken and bold supporters of American independence, he was a lawyer in Boston. In 1770, Adams took on the most difficult trial of his career: representing the British soldiers in the Boston Massacre.

Tension had been building in the city of Boston ever since the Stamp Act of 1765. Parliament had hoped to raise revenue by taxing the colonies, and the colonies resisted. Few places resented Britain's taxes and mercantilism more than in Boston, Massachusetts. In 1770, tensions broke out as a mob of Bostonians surrounded and threatened a group of British soldiers. The soldiers opened fire on the civilians, killing five people. The soldiers were to be tried in a Boston court, but no lawyer wanted to represent British soldiers—no one except John Adams, and here, in his final arguments before the jury, Adams explains to his audience, the jury, why his clients are innocent.

‖ JOHN ADAMS / 1735 - 1826

December 3-4, 1770

May it please your Honours and you Gentlemen of the Jury,

I am for the prisoners at the bar, and shall apologize for it only in the words of the Marquis Beccaria: "If I can but be the instrument of preserving one life, his blessing and tears of transport, shall be a sufficient consolation to me, for the contempt of all mankind."2 As the prisoners stand before you for their lives, it may be proper, to recollect with what temper the law requires we should proceed to this trial. The form of proceeding at their arraignment, has discovered that the spirit of the law upon such occasions, is conformable to humanity, to commonsense and feeling; that it is all benignity and candor. And the trial commences with the prayer of the Court, expressed by the Clerk, to the Supreme JUDGE of Judges, empires and worlds: "God send you a good deliverance."

We find, in the rules laid down by the greatest English Judges, who have been the brightest of mankind; We are to look upon it as more beneficial, that many guilty persons should escape unpunished, than one innocent person should suffer. The reason is, because it's of more importance to community, that innocence should be protected, than it is, that guilt should be punished; for guilt and crimes are so frequent in the world, that all of them cannot be punished; and many times they happen in such a manner, that it is not of much consequence to the public, whether they are punished or not. But when innocence itself, is brought to the bar and condemned, especially to die, the subject will exclaim, it is immaterial to me, whether I behave well or ill; for virtue itself, is no security. And if such a sentiment as this, should take place in the mind of the subject, there would be an end to all security what so ever. I will read the words of the law itself.

Adams reads from English law as it pertains to the case. Adams proceeds to cite examples when force may be used in self-defense or in similar instances, and then compare these principles to the events of the Boston Massacre.

"And so perhaps the killing of dangerous rioters, may be justified by any private persons, who cannot otherwise suppress them, or defend themselves from them; in as much as every private person seems to be authorized by the law, to arm himself for the purposes aforesaid." Hawkins p. 71. §1412—Here every private person is authorized to arm himself, and on the strength of this authority, I do not deny the inhabitants had a right to arm themselves at that time, for their defense, not for offence, that distinction is material and must be attended to.

Hawkins, page 75. §14. "And not only he who on an assault retreats to the wall or some such streight [*sic*], beyond which he can go no further, before he kills the other, is judged by the law to act upon unavoidable necessity; but also he who being assaulted in such a manner, and in such a place, that he cannot go back without manifestly endangering his life, kills the other

without retreating at all."13—§16. "And an officer who kills one that insults him in the execution of his office, and where a private person, that kills one who feloniously assaults him in the high way, may justify the fact without ever giving back at all." 14

There is no occasion for the Magistrate to read the Riot act. In the case before you, I suppose you will be satisfied when you come to examine the witnesses, and compare it with the rules of the common law, abstracted from all mutiny acts and articles of war, that these soldiers were in such a situation, that they could not help themselves; people were coming from Royal-exchange-lane, and other parts of the town, with clubs, and cord wood sticks; the soldiers were planted by the wall of the Custom House; they could not retreat, they were surrounded on all sides, for there were people behind them, as well as before them; there were a number of people in Royal-exchange-lane; the soldiers were so near to the Custom house, that they could not retreat, unless they had gone into the brick wall of it. I shall shew you presently, that all the party concerned in this unlawful design, were guilty of what any one of them did; if any body threw a snow-ball, it was the act of the whole party; if any struck with a club, or threw a club, and the club had killed any body, the whole party would have been guilty of murder in law.

Kinds of Oratory / Guided Notes

In the space provided, explain the *Occasion, the Chronological Focus, the Thematic Aim / Focus,* and the *Appeals* made in the previous speech.

Element	Student Work
Occasion	
Chronological Focus	
Thematic Aim / Focus	
Appeals	

Rhetorical Analysis / I have a Dream

Instructions: Our third speech comes from Martin Luther King Jr. (1929-1968). Martin Luther King Jr. was born in Atlanta, Georgia on January 15, 1929. King's impact on American history and his role in the Civil Rights movement can scarcely be underestimated. King grew up in the midst of segregation, in which black Americans had to attend separate facilities from those of whites including different schools, bathrooms, and water fountains, facilities that were supposedly "equal" but rarely, if ever, were. As part of his efforts in the Civil Rights movement, King organized boycotts against local bus companies and other businesses as part of an effort to overturn Jim Crow laws, an alternative name for segregation, and the policies that supported state-sponsored racism. In 1963, as support for equal rights for black Americans grew, King helped in part to organize one of the largest protests in American history: the March on Washington. On August 28, 1963, over 250,000 people gathered in Washington, DC in front of the Lincoln Memorial, where King delivered the following speech, appropriately entitled "I have a Dream."

‖ MARTIN LUTHER KING JR. / 1929 - 1968

August 28, 1963

I am happy to join with you today in what will go down in history as the greatest demonstration for freedom in the history of our nation. Five score years ago, a great American, in whose symbolic shadow we stand today, signed the Emancipation Proclamation. This momentous decree came as a great beacon light of hope to millions of Negro slaves who had been seared in the flames of withering injustice. It came as a joyous daybreak to end the long night of their captivity.

But one hundred years later, the Negro still is not free; one hundred years later, the life of the Negro is still sadly crippled by the manacles of segregation and the chains of discrimination; one hundred years later, the Negro lives on a lonely island of poverty in the midst of a vast ocean of material prosperity; one hundred years later, the Negro is still languished in the corners of American society and finds himself in exile in his own land.

So we've come here today to dramatize a shameful condition. In a sense we've come to our nation's capital to cash a check. When the architects of our republic wrote the magnificent words of the Constitution and the Declaration of Independence, they were signing a promissory note to which every American was to fall heir. This note was the promise that all men, yes, black men as well as white men, would be guaranteed the unalienable rights of life, liberty, and the pursuit of happiness.

It is obvious today that America has defaulted on this promissory note in so far as her citizens of color are concerned. Instead of honoring this sacred obligation, America has given the Negro people a bad check, a check which has come back marked "insufficient funds." But we refuse to believe that the bank of justice is bankrupt. We refuse to believe that there are insufficient funds in the great vaults of opportunity of this nation. And so we have come to cash this check, a check that will give us upon demand the riches of freedom and the security of justice.

We have also come to this hallowed spot to remind America of the fierce urgency of now. This is no time to engage in the luxury of cooling off or to take the tranquilizing drug of gradualism. Now is the time to make the real the promises of democracy; now is the time to rise from the dark and desolate valley of segregation to the sunlit path of racial justice; now is the time to lift our nation from the quicksands of racial injustice to the solid rock of brotherhood; now is the time to make justice a reality for all of God's children. It would be fatal for the nation to overlook the urgency of the moment. This sweltering summer of the Negro's legitimate discontent will not pass until there is an invigorating autumn of freedom and equality. Nineteen sixty-three is not an end, but a beginning. And those who hope that the Negro needed to blow off steam and will now be content, will have a rude awakening if the nation returns to business as usual. There will be neither rest nor tranquility in America until the Negro is granted his citizenship rights. The whirlwinds of revolt will continue to shake the foundations of our nation until the bright day of justice emerges.

But there is something that I must say to my people, who stand on the worn threshold which leads into the palace of justice. In the process of gaining our rightful place, we must not be guilty of wrongful deeds. Let us not seek to satisfy our thirst for freedom by drinking from the cup of bitterness and hatred. We must forever conduct our struggle on the high plane of dignity and discipline. We must not allow our creative protests to degenerate into physical violence. Again and again we must rise to the majestic heights of meeting physical force with soul force. The marvelous new militancy, which has engulfed the Negro community, must not lead us to a distrust of all white people. For many of our white brothers, as evidenced by their presence here today, have come to realize that their destiny is tied up with our destiny. And they have come to realize that their freedom is inextricably bound to our freedom. We cannot walk alone. And as we walk, we must make the pledge that we shall always march ahead. We cannot turn back.

There are those who are asking the devotees of Civil Rights, "When will you be satisfied?" We can never be satisfied as long as the Negro is the victim of the unspeakable horrors of police brutality; we can never be satisfied as long as our bodies, heavy with the fatigue of travel, cannot gain lodging in the motels of the highways and the hotels of the cities; we cannot be satisfied as long as the Negro's basic mobility is from a smaller ghetto to a larger one; we can never be satisfied as long as our children are stripped of their self-hood and robbed of their dignity by signs stating "For Whites Only"; we cannot be satisfied as long as the Negro in Mississippi cannot vote, and the Negro in New York believes he has nothing for which to vote. No! no, we are not satisfied, and we will not be satisfied until "justice rolls down like waters and righteousness like a mighty stream."

I am not unmindful that some of you have come here out of great trials and tribulations. Some of you have come fresh from narrow jail cells. Some of you have come from areas where your quest for freedom left you battered by the storms of persecution and staggered by the winds of police brutality. You have been the veterans of creative suffering. Continue to work with the faith that unearned suffering is redemptive. Go back to Mississippi. Go back to Alabama. Go back to South Carolina. Go back to Georgia. Go back to Louisiana. Go back to the slums and ghettos of our Northern cities knowing that somehow this situation can and will be changed. Let us not wallow in the valley of despair.

I say to you today, my friends, so even though we face the difficulties of today and tomorrow, I still have a dream. It is a dream deeply rooted in the American dream. I have a dream that one day this nation will rise up and live out the true meaning of its creed, "We hold these truths to be self-evident, that all men are created equal." I have a dream that one day on the red hills of Georgia, sons of former slaves and the sons of former slave owners will be able to sit down together at the table of brotherhood. I have a dream that one day even the state of Mississippi, a state sweltering with the heat of injustice, sweltering with the heat of oppression, will be transformed into an oasis of freedom and justice. I have a dream that my four little children will one day live in a nation where they will not be judged by the color of their skin but by the content of their character.

I HAVE A DREAM TODAY!

I have a dream that one day down in Alabama — with its vicious racists, with its Governor having his lips dripping with the words of interposition and nullification — one day right there in Alabama, little black boys and black girls will be able to join hands with little white boys and white girls as sisters and brothers.

I HAVE A DREAM TODAY!

I have a dream that one day every valley shall be exalted, and every hill and mountain shall be made low. The rough places will be plain and the crooked places will be made straight, "and the glory of the Lord shall be revealed, and all flesh shall see it together."

This is our hope. This is the faith that I go back to the South with. With this faith we will be able to hew out of the mountain of despair a stone of hope. With this faith we will be able to transform the jangling discords of our nation into a beautiful symphony of brother-hood.

With this faith we will be able to work together, to pray together, to struggle together, to go to jail together, to stand up for freedom together, knowing that we will be free one day. And this will be the day. This will be the day when all of God's children will be able to sing with new meaning, "My country 'tis of thee, sweet land of liberty, of thee I sing. Land where my father died, land of the pilgrim's pride, from every mountainside, let freedom ring." And if America is to be a great nation, this must become true.

So let freedom ring from the prodigious hilltops of New Hampshire; let freedom ring from the mighty mountains of New York; let freedom ring from the heightening Alleghenies of Pennsylvania; let freedom ring from the snow-capped Rockies of Colorado; let freedom ring from the curvaceous slopes of California. But not only that. Let freedom ring from Stone Mountain of Georgia; let freedom ring from Lookout Mountain of Tennessee; let freedom ring from every hill and mole hill of Mississippi. "From every mountainside, let freedom ring."

And when this happens, and when we allow freedom to ring, when we let it ring from every village and every hamlet, from every state and every city, we will be able to speed up that day when all of God's children, black men and white men, Jews and Gentiles, Protestants and Catholics, will be able to join hands and sing in the words of the old Negro spiritual: "Free at last. Free at last. Thank God Almighty, we are free at last."

ACTIVITY

Kinds of Oratory / Guided Notes

In the space provided, explain the *Occasion, the Chronological Focus, the Thematic Aim / Focus,* and the *Appeals* made in the previous speech.

Element	Student Work
Occasion	
Chronological Focus	
Thematic Aim / Focus	
Appeals	

Which speech best served as an example of deliberative oratory? Explain your reasoning and include references to the focus of the speech, themes, and the kinds of rhetorical appeals that the speaker made.

....

....

....

....

....

....

Which speech best served as an example of judicial oratory? Explain your reasoning and include references to the focus of the speech, themes, and the kinds of rhetorical appeals that the speaker made.

....

....

....

....

....

Which speech best served as an example of panegyric oratory? Explain your reasoning and include references to the focus of the speech, themes, and the kinds of rhetorical appeals that the speaker made.

Which speech was the most effective and why? Based on your summary reading of these three speeches, which speaker came the closest to becoming that ideal orator about which Quintilian writes?

Canon of Memory / **The Gettysburg Address**

Of the five canons, the canon of *memoria* may be the hardest canon to master. The practice of memorizing a speech requires considerable time and effort, but, like any skill, memorizing a speech becomes easier and easier the more things you try to memorize. We can use select speeches (like the one we just read) to practice our ability to memorize important passages and learn one method by which we can begin to memorize longer blocks of text. That method is to memorize one clause or sentence at a time, and then to go back and repeat *all of the sentences* you've memorized until you can recite the entire passage from memory.

> *Four score and seven years ago our fathers brought forth on this continent, a new nation, conceived in Liberty, and dedicated to the proposition that all men are created equal.*
>
> *Now we are engaged in a great civil war, testing whether that nation, or any nation so conceived and so dedicated, can long endure. We are met on a great battle-field of that war...*

Step and Description	Lines from Speech
Step 1: Read the first clause or sentence out loud upwards of five to ten times. Try to recite the sentence without looking at the words.	*Four score and seven years ago...*
Step 2: Read the next clause or sentence out loud upwards of five to ten times. Try to recite the sentence without looking at the words.	*Our fathers brought forth on this continent...*
Step 3: Go back to the beginning and repeat the first two clauses or sentences. Repeat until you have memorized the passage in question.	*Four score and seven years ago our fathers brought forth on this continent...*
Suggested Assignment: Recite the speech from memory for a homework, classwork, or assessment grade with one point for each word memorized (may also be taken as a percentage).	_____ / 272 points

ESSAY

Writing Prompt

In the space provided, what was the most valuable concept or idea you learned about in this chapter? Why *that* idea or concept, and not another? If you have had opportunities to speak in public before, how might have the material in this chapter helped you? Reflect, too, on the speech(es) provided in this chapter: why did the ideas and goals communicated in the speech matter, and how did the speaker go about trying to persuade the audience to believe in them?

U.S. HOUSE OF REPRESENTATIVES CHAMBER

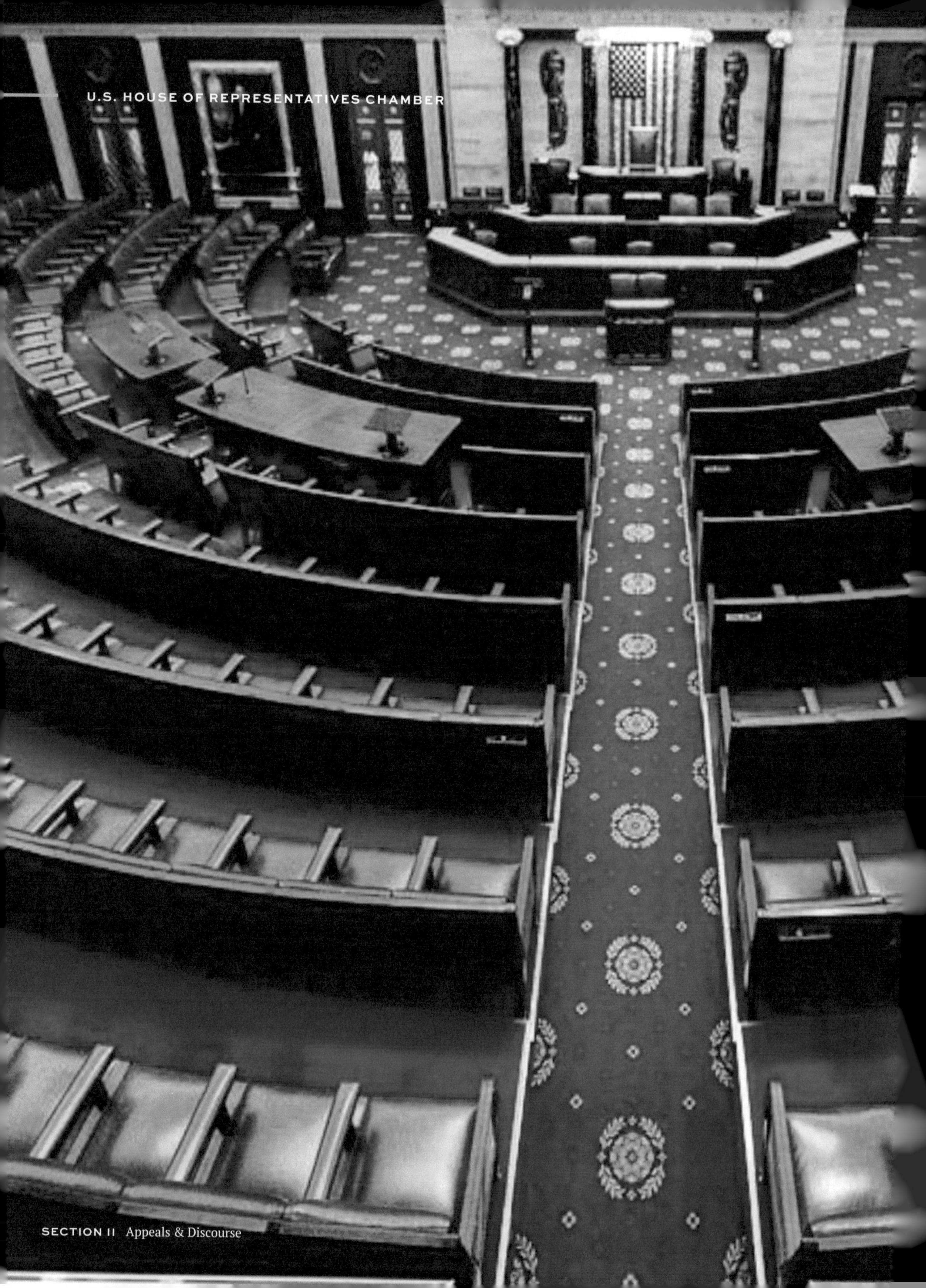

CHAPTER

The Six Parts of Discourse

ROADMAP

- ✦ Learn about the six parts of discourse.

- ✦ Learn how to identify and evaluate major section breaks in a speech.

- ✦ Read selections from Daniel Webster's *Second Reply to Hayne*.

THALES
OUTCOME

Nº 10

A person with a **Strong Work Ethic** *critiques components of his/her work ethic including resilience, reliability, and honesty.*

The *Six Parts of Discourse* focuses on writing an outline of your speech. The task of writing is hard enough as it is, but writing an outline and mapping out your points ahead of time makes this process much easier and more efficient. Teachers of classical rhetoric identified the *Six Parts of Discourse* as the six components that should be present in every speech, although gifted orators have some flexibility in the order of their points.

The Six Parts of Discourse

THE SECOND OF THE five canons of rhetoric is the **dispositio**. The *dispositio* is the *disposition*, the *arrangement* or the *organization* of the material in a speech. In other words, the *dispositio* focuses on how an orator should structure his speech, paper, or some other meaningful, creative work of communication to deliver it with maximum efficiency. Once you know how you want to argue your case, and how you want to support that idea, you want to organize your material so that your material will be as effective and persuasive as possible. Aristotle considered only two real parts to a speech: the statement of a case and the proof of a case. An orator might state their case, and then provide the supporting evidence to prove their case. Latin authors built upon Aristotle's initial framework by dividing the *dispositio* into six parts, called the **Six Parts of Discourse**. They are as follows:

Exordium: The introduction of a speech.

Narratio: The speaker explains or states the case under discussion.

Divisio: The speaker presents an outline of the points in the speech.

Confirmatio: The speaker presents a proof of the case.

Confutatio: The speaker presents and refutes the opposing arguments.

Peroratio: The conclusion to a speech.

The structure provides a helpful outline upon which you can adorn your thoughts. Any good speech will begin with a stirring introduction (*Exordium*). Then the orator states their case (*Narratio*); highlights points in support of their case (*Divisio*); weaves confirmation of the case throughout the speech (*Confirmatio*) and, as needed, cites opposing arguments and refutes them as needed (*Confutatio*). Then, once the orator has successfully advanced and defended the main idea, the only thing left is to wrap up the main points of the speech with a meaningful sendoff in the conclusion (*Peroratio*).

Quintilian posed these questions when thinking about the arrangement of the material:

* *When is an introduction necessary, and when can it be omitted or abbreviated?*

The Six Parts of Discourse provide a helpful way to arrange and organize your material, but, as Quintilian recommends, an orator must use his judgment to know how best to arrange the material in his speech.

Vocabulary

Write down this vocabulary in your notebook. These terms will help you better learn and understand the material in this chapter.

Dispositio
The disposition, the "arrangement" or the "organization" of the material in a speech.

Six Parts of Discourse
The division of a speech into different parts, including the introduction, the statement of the case, answers to opposing arguments, and the conclusion of the speech.

Exordium
The introduction to a speech.

Narratio
The speaker explains the nature of his case and why he is speaking.

Divisio
The speaker presents an outline of the points in his argument.

Confirmatio
The speaker presents proof, evidence, and examples that support his overarching point.

Confutatio
The speaker addresses the opposing arguments that may be raised against his speech.

Peroratio
The conclusion of a speech.

QUINTILIAN / AD 35 - 100
Roman educator and author of the Institutes of Oratory

- *When should we make our statement of facts continuous and when should we break it up?*

- *Under what circumstances can we omit the statement of facts altogether?*

- *When should we begin by dealing with the arguments advanced by our opponents? When we should we begin by proposing our own arguments?*

- *When is it advisable to present your strongest argument first—or contra, your weakest arguments?*

- *Which of our arguments will our audience readily accept? Where might they need some persuading? Should we attempt to refute our opponents arguments in whole or in detail?*

- *How much ethical appeal must we exert in order to conciliate the audience?*

- *Should we reserve our emotional appeals for the conclusion or distribute them throughout the discourse? What evidence or documents should we use? When will they be most effective?*

The six parts of discourse are a helpful tool to help you begin thinking about your speech or your paper and the most effective means to argue for it. As with other components of rhetoric and oratory, the key is to devote the amount of time needed to research, reflect, write, and edit your topic so that your work is as effective and eloquent as it can possibly be.

Rhetorical Analysis / Second Reply to Hayne

Instructions: Read over the selection from Daniel Webster's *Second Reply to Hayne* and identify the breaks in his outline. Each of those breaks corresponds to one of the *six parts of discourse*.

Despite its non-descriptive title, Webster's *Second Reply to Hayne* happens to be one of the most famous and significant speeches from the early American republic. Daniel Webster lived from 1782 to 1852 and served as senator from Massachusetts, forming something of a triumvirate with senators Henry Clay of Kentucky and John C. Calhoun of South Carolina. All three senators believed the United States of America possessed practically limitless potential thanks to its natural resources, seemingly endless supply of land, and the hardworking, virtuous character of the American people. They believed in a strong federal government, one capable of building roads and canals to link disparate American markets together, and in a strong military, one capable of defending American commercial interests at home and abroad. To Webster, this idea was summed up in the idea of the American union, a solid bond between the federal government and the American people.

Soon, the triumvirate fell apart. John C. Calhoun realized that the interests of his home state of South Carolina ran contrary to the idea of a strong federal government. The kind of union America would be also affected the issues of slavery, American expansion, and tariffs, additional charges on imported goods that benefited Northern business interests at the expense of the Southern states. And so the debates raged in the U.S. Senate, with Daniel Webster debating with Robert Hayne of South Carolina, an ally of Calhoun, over the future of the American republic.

January 19-27, 1830

Mr. President - When the mariner has been tossed for many days in thick weather, and on an unknown sea, he naturally avails himself of the first pause in the storm, the earliest glance of the sun, to take his latitude, and ascertain how far the elements have driven him from his true course. Let us imitate this prudence, and, before we float farther on the waves of this debate, refer to the point from which we departed, that we may at least be able to conjecture where we now are. I ask for the reading of the resolution before the Senate.

The Secretary read the resolution, as follows:

Resolved, *That the Committee on Public Lands be instructed to inquire and report the quantity of public lands remaining unsold within each State and Territory, and whether it be expedient to limit for a certain period the sales of the public lands to such lands only as have been heretofore been offered for sale, and are now subject to entry at the minimum price. And, also, whether the office of Surveyor-General, and some of the land offices, may not be abolished without detriment to the public interest; or whether it be expedient to adopt measures to hasten the sales and extend more rapidly the surveys of the public lands.*

We have thus heard, Sir, what the resolution is which is actually before us for consideration; and it will readily occur to every one, that it is almost the only subject about which something has not been said in the speech, running through two days, by which the Senate has been entertained by the gentleman from South Carolina. Every topic in the wide range of our public affairs, whether past or present—every thing, general or local, whether belonging to national politics or party politics—seems to have attracted more or less of the honorable member's attention, save only the resolution before the Senate. He has spoken of every thing but the public lands; they have escaped his notice. To that subject, in all his excursions, he has not paid even the cold respect of a passing glance...

Sir, let me recur to pleasing recollections; let me indulge in refreshing remembrance of the past; let me remind you that, in early times, no States cherished greater harmony, both of principle and feeling, than Massachusetts and South Carolina. Would to God that harmony might again return! Shoulder to shoulder they went through the Revolution, hand in hand they stood round the administration of Washington, and felt his own great arm lean on them for support. Unkind feeling, if it exist, alienation, and distrust are the growth, unnatural to such soils, of false principles since sown. They are weeds, the seeds of which that same great arm never scattered.

Mr. President ,I shall enter on no encomium upon Massachusetts; she needs none. There she is. Behold her, and judge for yourselves. There is her history; the world knows it by heart. The past, at least, is secure. There is Boston, and Concord, and Lexington, and Bunker Hill; and there they will remain for ever. The bones of her sons, falling in the great struggle for Independence, now lie mingled with the soil of every State from New England to Georgia; and there they will lie for ever. And Sir, where American Liberty raised its first voice, and where its youth was nurtured and sustained, there it still lives, in the strength of its manhood, and full of its original spirit. If discord and disunion shall wound it, if party strife and blind ambition shall hawk at and tear it, if folly and madness, if uneasiness under salutary and necessary restraint, shall succeed in separating it from that Union, by which alone its existence is made sure, it will stand, in the end, by the side of that cradle in which its infancy was rocked; over the friends who gather round it; and it will fall at last, if fall it must,

|| DANIEL WEBSTER / 1782 - 1852

amidst the proudest monuments of its own glory, and on the very spot of its origin.

There yet remains to be performed, Mr. President, by far the most grave and important duty, which I feel to be devolved on me by this occasion. It is to state, and to defend, what I conceive to be the true principles of the Constitution under which we are here assembled. I might well have desired that so weighty a task should have fallen into other and abler hands. I could have wished that it should have been executed by those whose character and experience give weight and influence to their opinions, such as cannot possibly belong to mine. But, Sir, I have met the occasion, not sought it; and I shall proceed to state my own sentiments, without challenging for them any particular regard, with studied plainness, and as much precision as possible. I understand the honorable gentleman from South Carolina to maintain, that it is a right of the State legislatures to interfere, whenever, in their judgment, this government transcends its constitutional limits, and to arrest the operation of its laws.

I understand him to maintain this right, as a right existing under the Constitution, not as a right to overthrow it on the ground of extreme necessity, such as would justify violent revolution.

I understand him to maintain an authority, on the part of the States, thus to interfere, for the purpose of correcting the exercise of power by the general government, of checking it, and of compelling it to conform to their opinion of the extend of its powers.

I understand him to maintain that the ultimate power of judging of the constitutional extent of its own authority is not lodged exclusively in the general government, or any branch of it: but that, on the contrary, the States may lawfully decide for themselves, and each State for itself, whether, in a given case, the act of the general government transcends its power.

I understand him to insist, that, if the exigency of the case, in the opinion of any State government, require it, such State government may, by its own sovereign authority, annul an act of the general government which it deems plainly and palpably unconstitutional.

This is the sum of what I understand from him to be the South Carolina doctrine, and the doctrine which he maintains. I propose to consider it, and compare it with the Constitution. Allow me to say, as a preliminary remark, that I call this the South Carolina doctrine only because the gentleman himself has so denominated it. I do not feel at liberty to say that South Carolina, as a State, has ever advanced these sentiments. I hope she has not, and never may. That a great majority of her people are opposed to the tariff laws, is doubtless true. That a majority, somewhat less than that just mentioned, conscientiously believe that these laws are unconstitutional, may probably also be true. But that any majority holds the right of direct State interference at State discretion, the right of nullifying acts of Congress by acts of State legislation, is more than I know, and what I shall be slow to believe...

This leads us to inquire into the origin of this government and the source of its power. Whose agent is it? Is

WEBSTER'S SECOND REPLY TO HAYNE
Painting by George P.A. Healy (~1850).

it the creature of the State legislatures, or the creature of the people? If the government of the United States be the agent of the State governments, then they may control it, provided they can agree in the manner of controlling it; if it be the agent of the people, then the people alone can control it, restrain it, modify, or reform it.

It is observable enough, that the doctrine for which the honorable gentleman contends leads him to the necessity of maintaining, not only that this general government is the creature of the States, but that it is the creature of each of the States severally, so that each may deign the power for itself of determining whether it acts within the limits of its authority. It is the servant of four-and-twenty masters, of different will and different purposes and yet bound to obey all. This absurdity (for it seems no less) arises from a misconception as to the origin of this government and its true character. It is, Sir, the people's Constitution, the people's government, made for the people, made by the people, and answerable to the people. The people of the United States have declared that the Constitution shall be the supreme law. We must either admit the proposition, or dispute their authority. The States are, unquestionably, sovereign, so far as their sovereignty is not affected by this supreme law. But the State legislatures, as political bodies, however sovereign, are yet not sovereign over the people. So far as the people have given the power to the general government, so far the grant is unquestionably good, and the government holds of the people, and not of the State governments. We are all agents of the same supreme power, the people. The general government and the State governments derive their authority from the same source. Neither can, in relation to the other, be called primary, though one is definite and restrict-ed, and the other general and residuary. The national government possesses those powers which it will be shown the people have conferred upon it, and no more. All the rest belongs to the State governments, or to the people themselves. So far as the people have restrained State sovereignty, by the expression of their will, in the Constitution of the United States, so far, it must be admitted. State sovereignty is effectually controlled. I do not contend that it is, or ought to be, controlled farther. The sentiment to which I have referred propounds that State sovereignty is only to be controlled by its own "feeling of justice": that is to say, it is not to be controlled at all, for one who is to follow his own feelings is under no legal control.

Now, however men may think this ought to be, the fact is, that the people of the United States have chosen to impose control on State sovereignties. There are those, doubtless, who wish they had been left without restraint; but the Constitution has ordered the matter differently. To make war, for instance, is an exercise of sovereignty; but the Constitution declares that no State shall make war. To coin money is another exercise of sovereign power, but no State is at liberty to coin money. Again, the Constitution says that no sovereign State shall be so sovereign as to make a treaty. These prohibitions, it must be confessed, are a control on the State sovereignty of South Carolina, as

well as of the other States, which does not arise "from her own feelings of honorable justice." The opinion referred to, therefore, is in defiance of the plainest provisions of the Constitution...

I must now beg to ask, Sir, Whence is this supposed right of the States derived? Where do they find the power to interfere with the laws of the Union? Sir the opinion which the honorable gentleman maintains is a notion founded in a total misapprehension, in my judgment, of the origin of this government, and of the foundation on which it stands. I hold it to be a popular government, erected by the people; those who admin-ister it, responsible to the people; and itself capable of being amended and modified, just as the people may choose it should be. It is as popular, just as truly emanating from the people, as the State governments. It is created for one purpose; the State governments for another. It has its own powers; they have theirs. There is no more authority with them to arrest the operation of a law of Congress, than with Congress to arrest the operation of their laws. We are here to administer a Constitution emanating immediately from the people, and trusted by them to our administration.

It is not the creature of the State governments. It is of no moment to the argument, that certain acts of the State legislatures are necessary to fill our seats in this body. That is not one of their original State powers, a part of the sovereignty of the State. It is a duty which the people, by the Constitution itself, have imposed on the State legislatures; and which they might have left to be performed elsewhere, if they had seen fit. So they have left the choice of President with electors; but all this does not affect the proposition that this whole government, President, Senate, and House of Repre-sentatives, is a popular government. It leaves it still all its popular character. The governor of a State (in some of the States) is chosen, not directly by the people, but by those who are chosen by the people, for the purpose of performing, among other duties, that of electing a governor. Is the government of the State, on that account, not a popular government? This government, Sir, is the independent offspring of the popular will. It is not the creature of State legislatures; nay, more, if the whole truth must be told, the people brought it into existence, established it, and have hitherto supported it, for the very purpose, amongst others, of imposing certain salutary restraints on State sovereignties. The States cannot now make war; they cannot contract alliances; they cannot make, each for itself, separate regulations of commerce; they cannot lay imposts; they cannot coin money. If this Constitution, Sir, be the creature of State legislatures, it must be admitted that it has obtained a strange control over the volitions of its creators.

The people, then, Sir, erected this government. They gave it a Constitution, and in that Constitution they have enumerated the powers which they bestow on it. They have made it a limited government. They have defined its authority. They have restrained it to the exercise of such powers as are granted; and all others, they declare, are reserved to the States or the people. But, Sir, they have not stopped here. If they had, they would have accomplished but half their work. No definition can be so clear, as to avoid possibility of doubt; no limitation so precise, as to exclude all uncertainty. Who, then, shall construe this grant of the people? Who shall interpret their will, where it may be supposed they have left it doubtful? With whom do they repose this ultimate right of deciding on the powers of government? Sir, they have settled all this in the fullest manner. They have left it with the government itself, in its appropriate branches. Sir, the very chief end, the main design, for which the whole Constitution was framed and adopted, was to establish a government that should not be obliged to act through State agency, or depend on State opinion and State discretion. The people had had quite enough of that kind of government under the Confederation. Under

that system, the legal action, the application of law to individuals, belonged exclusively to the States. Congress could only recommend; their acts were not of binding force, till the States had adopted and sanctioned them. Are we in that condition still? Are we yet at the mercy of State discretion and State construction? Sir, if we are, then vain will be our attempt to maintain the Constitution under which we sit.

But, Sir, the people have wisely provided, in the Constitution itself, a proper, suitable mode and tribunal for settling questions of Constitutional law. There are in the Constitution grants of powers to Congress, and restrictions on these powers. There are, also, prohibitions on the States. Some authority must, therefore, necessarily exist, having the ultimate jurisdiction to fix and ascertain the interpretation of these grants, restrictions, and prohibitions. The Constitution has itself pointed out, ordained, and established that authority. How has it accomplished this great and essential end? By declaring, Sir, that "the Constitution, and the laws of the United States made in pursuance thereof, shall be the supreme law of the land, any thing in the constitution or laws of any State to the contrary notwithstanding."

This, Sir, was the first great step. By this the supremacy of the Constitution and laws of the United States is declared. The people so will it. No State law is to be valid which comes in conflict with the Constitution, or any law of the United States passed in pursuance of it. But who shall decide this question of interference? To whom lies the last appeal? This, Sir, the Constitution itself decides also, by declaring, "That the judicial power shall extend to all cases arising under the Constitution and laws of the United States." These two provisions cover the whole ground. They are, in truth, the keystone of the arch! With these it is a government; without them it is a confederation. In pursuance of these clear and express provisions, Congress established, at its very first session, in the judicial act, a mode for carrying them into full effect, and for bringing all questions of constitutional power to the final decision of the Supreme Court. It then, Sir, became a government. It then had the means of self-protection; and but for this, it would, in all probability, have been now among things which are past. Having constituted the government, and declared its powers, the people have further said, that, since somebody must decide on the extent of these powers, the government shall itself decide; subject always, like other popular governments, to its responsibility to the people...

I have not allowed myself, Sir, to look beyond the Union, to see what might lie hidden in the dark recess behind. I have not coolly weighed the chances of preserving liberty when the bonds that unite us together shall be broken asunder. I have not accustomed myself to hang over the precipice of disunion, to see whether, with my short sight, I can fathom the depth of the abyss below; nor could I regard him as a safe counselor in the affairs of this government, whose thoughts should be mainly bent on considering, not how the Union may be best preserved, but how tolerable might be the condition of the people when it should be broken up and destroyed. While the Union lasts, we have high, exciting, gratifying prospects spread out before us and our children. Beyond that I seek not to penetrate the veil. God grant that in my day, at least, that curtain may not rise! God grant that on my vision never may be opened what lies behind! When my eyes shall be turned to behold for the last time the sun in heaven, may I not see him shining on the broken and dishonored fragments of a once glorious Union; on States dissevered, discordant, belligerent; on a land rent with civil feuds, or drenched, it may be, in fraternal blood! Let their last feeble and lingering glance rather behold the gorgeous ensign of the republic, now known and honored throughout the earth, still full high advanced, its arms and trophies streaming in their original luster, not a stripe erased or polluted, not a single star obscured, bearing for its motto, no such miserable interrogatory as "What is all this worth?" nor those other words of delusion and folly, "Liberty first and Union afterwards"; but everywhere, spread all over in characters of living light, blazing on all its ample folds, as they float over the sea and over the land, and in every wind under the whole heavens, that other sentiment, dear to every true American heart—Liberty and Union, now and for ever, one and inseparable!

What issue initially sparked this debate? Beyond that immediate issue, what larger issues are at stake here? For context, refer to the Resolution as read by the Secretary in the second paragraph of the speech.

....

....

....

....

....

....

Webster provides several counterarguments to the arguments Robert Hayne had supplied in his speech. Summarize two of those counter arguments here. Why does Webster go to such difficulties to recreate his opponent's argument?

....

....

....

....

....

Daniel Webster argues that, ultimately, the federal government holds the appropriate jurisdiction when it comes western land grants and other issues. What reasons does he cite in support of this position?

....

....

....

....

....

....

What does the "union" of the federal government ultimately rest on?

....

....

....

....

....

....

....

Rhetorical Analysis / Second Reply to Hayne

Instructions: In the space provided, answer the following questions concerning the purpose, audience, and tone of the speech. These criteria will help you identify the kind of rhetorical appeals used in the speech. Answer in complete sentences.

Criteria	Description
## The Purpose of the Speech *Why did the orator deliver this speech? What was his goal?*	
## The Audience of the Speech *Who was the audience? What was the occasion?*	
## The Tone of the Speech *Tone is the way that an orator or an author feels about his work and the subject at hand.* *How does the speaker feel about the subject he is speaking about?*	

Six Parts of Discourse / **Second Reply to Hayne**

Instructions: In the table below, we have provided excerpts from Daniel Webster's *Second Reply to Hayne*. Identify which of the *Six Parts of Discourse* to which each section belongs. Then, explain your reasoning in the space provided in the third column. Each part is used only once; choose from the list below.

Exordium	Narratio	Divisio	Confirmatio	Confutatio	Peroratio

Selection from Second Reply to Hayne	Part of Discourse	Explanation
Mr. President - When the mariner has been tossed for many days in thick weather, and on an unknown sea, he naturally avails himself of the first pause in the storm, the earliest glance of the sun, to take his latitude, and ascertain how far the elements have driven him from his true course...		
I understand the honorable gentleman from South Carolina to maintain, that it is a right of the State legislatures to interfere, whenever, in their judgment, this government transcends its constitutional limits, and to arrest the operation of its laws...		
in every wind under the whole heavens, that other sentiment, dear to every true American heart— Liberty and Union, now and for ever, one and inseparable!		

Six Parts of Discourse / Second Reply to Hayne

Instructions: Continue the exercise from the previous page, identifying each of the *Six Parts of Discourse* next to the quotation drawn from the speech. Explain your reasoning in the space provided in the third column. Each part is used only once; choose from the list below.

Exordium	*Narratio*	*Divisio*	*Confirmatio*	*Confutatio*	*Peroratio*

Selection from **Second Reply to Hayne**	Part of Discourse	Explanation
It is, Sir, the people's Constitution, the people's government, made for the people, made by the people, and answerable to the people. The people of the United States have declared that the Constitution shall be the supreme law...		
There yet remains to be performed, Mr. President, by far the most grave and important duty, which I feel to be devolved on me by this occasion. It is to state, and to defend, what I conceive to be the true principles of the Constitution under which we are here assembled...		
Of the Six Parts of Discourse, *it seems as if Webster neglected to include one part. Which part was it? Why might Webster have neglected this part?*		

The Goal of Rhetoric

ROADMAP

✦ Learn about the goal and purpose of rhetoric in light of the value of truth-telling and personal integrity.

✦ Learn about the life and example of Socrates and his conflict with the Sophists.

✦ Learn about the value of a liberal arts education, an education focused on books, ideas, and subjects that are worth studying in and of themselves and not for the sake of something else.

THALES
OUTCOME

№ 1

A person of **Unfailing Integrity** *exemplifies integrity while developing trusting relationships.*

The Greek philosopher Socrates wanted to know what was true, good, and beautiful in hopes that this understanding would help him to become a better, more virtuous individual. The purpose of rhetoric is not merely to become a better, more effective communicator, but to become better at identifying what is true and good and persuading others to choose what is good, true, and beautiful, too.

The Telos of Rhetoric

NOW MORE THAN EVER, THE MODERN world needs individuals committed to what is good, what is true, and what is beautiful. Yet, many people dismiss the value of rhetoric and the need to learn the art of public speaking, even going so far as to contend that oratory is irrelevant for one's professional career. On the other hand, some people claim that rhetoric and public speaking are important tools for self-advancement and success, but they should really be used to advance one's interests and not that of the greater good. After all, what good ever came from someone giving a speech? So, if rhetoric and public speaking have a purpose, what is it? Thankfully, **Socrates** has an answer for that question. We can find many valuable answers to this issue by looking at the dispute between Socrates and his followers on the one hand and a group of professional teachers called the **Sophists** on the other.

Socrates was a philosopher who lived in the city of **Athens** from 470 to 399 BC. He worked as a stone-cutter until the **Oracle at Delphi** pronounced him to be the *wisest man in Greece*. From then on, Socrates went around Athens asking people about the nature of wisdom and encouraging them to pursue philosophy and virtue. Socrates gathered a number of students who followed him around Athens and listened to his teaching; chief amongst them was **Plato**, who lived from around 428 to 347 BC. It is Plato who wrote down much of Socrates' teaching in over forty books known as **dialogues**.

On the other hand, the Sophists taught their students how to speak well in public but with little regard for the truth. The Sophists were a group of rhetoricians who traveled around the Greek world teaching students the art of public speaking for huge fees. Socrates took issue with the Sophists because of the degree to which the Sophists abused rhetoric and oratory for personal enrichment. On the whole, the Sophists did not care about the cultivation of wisdom or truth, and they taught their students how to gloss over their lack of knowledge with oratorical tricks. The Sophists and their students learned how to make bad arguments appear good and how to dissemble the truth, not seek out the truth.

In Plato's *Gorgias*, Socrates speaks with one such Sophist, Gorgias of Leontinoi (483-375 BC). Socrates calls oratory a *knack,* an activity that produces "a

BIG IDEA

The Greek word telos *refers to the goal or purpose of anything. As far as the goal of rhetoric, we should use the knowledge and skill we have gained in public speaking to cultivate a deep and abounding confidence in things that are true, good, and beautiful and to encourage those around us to do the same.*

Vocabulary

Write down this vocabulary in your notebook. These terms will help you better learn and understand the material in this chapter.

Socrates

A Greek philosopher and "gadfly of Athens" whose incessant question and probing into the nature of the good life led to his execution in 399 BC. He lived from 470 to 399 BC.

Sophists

A group of teachers of rhetoric who taught wealthy Athenians how to speak well in public. They did not have much, if any, regard for the truth.

Athens

A city in ancient Greece that, thanks to its wealth, its civic freedoms, and figures like Socrates, Plato, and Aristotle, was the birthplace of philosophy, democracy, and other components of the Western tradition.

Oracle at Delphi

The Greek world had a number of oracles who gave pronouncements about the future; the Oracle at Delphi was among the most famous.

Plato

A student of Socrates, Plato's writings serve as the basis for much of Western philosophy. He lived from around 428 to 347 BC.

Dialogue

A literary work where two or more speakers discuss a topic of philosophical significance.

THE FINAL MOMENTS OF SOCRATES
The Death of Socrates *by Jacques-Louis David (1789)*

certain gratification and pleasure" and is on a level with baking cookies. This is because both oratory and baking mimic the appearance and the essence of what is good without actually being good or even being knowledgeable on that subject at all. In the same manner that a child confuses cookies for good, healthy food because of the cookies' sweet taste, so an audience can be tricked by a talented orator who can speak well but knows nothing else of his subject. Socrates says,

> *Oratory doesn't need to have any knowledge of the state of their subject matters; it only needs to have discovered some device to produce persuasion in order to make itself appear to those who don't have knowledge that it knows more than those who actually do have it.*

In pastry baking, that "device" is sugar; in oratory, it is rhetorical devices, the topics, the modes of persuasion—effectively all the skills we have covered in this book.

But Socrates' contention is not with rhetoric *per se* but with the Sophists' selfish manipulation of rhetoric. Socrates devoted himself to the cultivation

CHAPTER 09 The Goal of Rhetoric + 145

of wisdom and the pursuit of truth, the divine mission the Oracle of Delphi gave him in pronouncing him the "wisest man" in Athens. The Sophists, meanwhile, had no regard for the truth and made their students worse individuals by teaching them to speak eloquently and gloss over their lack of both knowledge and morals. Oratory is a tool, and Socrates was indignant that the Sophists used this tool to benefit themselves and not others. The problem is not with oratory, but with a disregard for the truth.

But one should never separate oratory from truth. Per Quintilian, the ideal orator was as committed to virtue and wisdom as he or she was an eloquent, persuasive, and dynamic public speaker. One can think of Cicero, the paragon of eloquence and a model for disinterested civic virtue. Cicero not only reached the heights of oratory, but used his gifts to denounce the tyranny of Marc Antony, for which Marc Antony would execute this venerable Roman statesman. We should still learn the art and the skills of public speaking, but we should be especially careful that we use these tools with a heightened sense of empathy and concern for the needs of others, not merely to advance our own agendas.

The modern world, meanwhile, contends that oratory and public speaking are simply irrelevant to one's professional goals. The marketplace requires students to be well-versed in coding, engineering, and the practical sciences, and the time needed to master these fields necessitates that students spend less time on humanities—public speaking included. It is all well and good to have read Plato or Dante, but the job market requires hard skills that take considerable time for students to master. Firms will pass over the applicants that do not possess them, so what should our students do?

We should bear in mind several important items when we consider the role and the purpose of education.

First, we should consider how powerful the human mind really is. Per Quintilian, the human mind is capable of undertaking a series of interrelated tasks all at once, and one's intellectual abilities do not diminish but rather expand to meet these challenges. The difficult skill of coding is not hampered by learning Greek or Latin or memorizing speeches. The elements of a Classical education in general, and rhetoric in particular, make it easier to learn difficult subjects like coding, as the mind grows accustomed to learning systems of information that require careful precision in their application.

The point of a liberal arts education is not merely to prepare students for their professional career, but for life. The *liberal* in liberal arts refers to the freedom we enjoy, the free time we devote to our education, and in the responsible ways we use the freedom we have been given. A liberal arts education is meant to prepare students for the myriad challenges that accompany daily living above and beyond the practical skills demanded by their jobs. Classical education in general and rhetoric in particular are meant to help students develop the strong, stalwart character needed to take on difficult challenges in the world today.

Lastly, public speaking is far more crucial to one's professional success than you think. Job applicants need certain hard skills when they first arrive at a company, and while they need to develop more skills the longer they work there, at a certain point those workers become managers. Then, they are supervising the work of new employees with the most up-to-date and advanced skill sets. As you progress in your career, those hard technical skills will most likely decrease in importance while your ability to lead and manage people increases. As a result, you should have a network of skills that includes a mix of visionary leadership, business acumen, and public speaking, because leaders that cannot communicate and cast a vision for their organizations will not stay in leadership for very long. The ability to speak well in public is often the trademark of bold, visionary leaders; thus, the art of oratory is one of the most valuable skills you can develop.

The goal of classical education in general and of rhetoric in particular is to prepare you for life. This preparation requires not only the skills that allow you to be successful, but also to develop the moral character needed to navigate challenges that accompany everyday life. The orator may be widely read and possess the ability to think quickly on his feet, but to be a good public speaker, the orator has to be a moral individual committed to finding the true, just course of action, and then successfully convince the members of his audience to pursue that course. If trivium is the place where the *three roads* of grammar, logic, and rhetoric meet, those three roads culminate in students who can not only think well but also live well. They are good, moral individuals who value the opportunity to cultivate virtue in themselves and in the people they care about, and they have developed such character that they can both choose what is good and persuade others to pursue what is good, what is true, and what is beautiful, too. Rhetoric, then, can channel these concerns into leaders who not only know what is right, and have the integrity to do what is right, but also the eloquence to exhort others to choose what is right. Quintilian says that rhetoric allows individuals of virtue not merely "to speak or plead, but as was the case with Pericles, to hurl forth lightning and thunder" (104).

Who was Socrates, and what did he seek after as a philosopher?

Who were the Sophists, and why were the Sophists in so much conflict with Socrates?

What is the telos or the goal and purpose of rhetoric?

Writing Prompt

In the space provided, think back on everything you have learned this year. *How have you grown as a result of being classically educated, grown not only in knowledge and skills but also character and virtue?*

APPENDIX

Appendix

ROADMAP

+ A suggested rubric for formal writing assignments.

+ A suggested rubric for in-class presentations.

+ A *Socratic Seminar* prep sheet and conversation map to help students practice the skills of analytical reading. Teachers may give this prep sheet to students to complete as they are reading the primary source texts.

Essay Rubric

To help us to think more clearly, we will spend considerable time this quarter writing expository essays based on the texts we read in class. These expository essays are descriptive in nature and answer one question that arises from the material we are reading in class. Essentially, an expository essay is one that explains. In an expository essay, the writer seeks to explain by reading and rereading the text under analysis to better explain that author's argument and the consequences of their ideas. Each essay will be graded according to the following rubric (see below).

Essay Component	Criteria
Introduction 5 points per criterion ____ / 25 points	____ Hook ____ Background Information of Time Period/Author/ Philosophical Problem ____ Context, in terms of the author's background, the main idea of the text, the problem the author is trying to solve, etc. ____ Underlined Thesis statement (a debatable claim that contains 1 to 2 reasons why that claim is correct) ____ MLA Format (Heading, Double Spaced, etc.)
Body Paragraph 5 points per criterion ____ / 20 points	____ Hook (short, pithy, includes language from thesis statement) ____ Evidence (specific examples from reading, quotations from text, etc.) ____ Explanation / Analysis / Synthesis (the significance of this information in light of the student's thesis) ____ Transition
Conclusion 5 points per criterion ____ / 15 points	____ Synthesis of Main Points ____ Restatement of Thesis ____ Meaningful Send-Off to Reader

TOTAL: ____ / 60 POINTS

Presentation Rubric

The third way of the trivium is *rhetoric*, the art of public speaking. In the ancient world, public speaking was equated with public service and leadership, for the speaker recognized the best course of action for his city and had to bring together the words, thoughts, and arguments to deliver a speech that fit whatever the occasion called for. Rhetoric encompassed all the skills needed to argue rightly on a subject and compose a speech that is logically sound, aesthetically pleasing, and powerfully delivered so that the audience is inspired to take up the course of action expounded upon by the orator. As a result, we will spend time this year writing and delivering speeches and developing our ability to speak persuasively.

Presentation Component	Criteria
Content of Speech 5 points per criterion ____ / 20 points	____ Student presents a clear, defensible and persuasive claim. ____ Thesis is defended with clear rhetoric, interesting and engaging word choices, and is clearly threaded logically and precisely throughout the entire presentation. ____ Student presents clear and accurate ideas in support of his/her thesis. ____ The thesis topic arises out of the events, figures, and ideas of the Western tradition.
Presentation 5 points per criterion ____ / 20 points	____ Student holds attention of the audience with eye contact ____ Student displays has appropriate and professional movements (standing upright with a confident demeanor). ____ Student speaks with engaging tone of voice, interesting inflections for key points, and outstanding pacing. ____ The presentation is enthusiastic, relevant, and engaging.
Visual Aids and Preparation 5 points per criterion ____ / 20 points	____ Student presents a clear, attractive and professional visual presentation free of errors. ____ The presentation includes consistent, easy to read font choices. ____ Text and images are always centered, aligned, and consistent. ____ Student chooses harmonious and appealing style, color, and template choices.

TOTAL: ____ / 60 POINTS

Socratic Seminar Prep Sheet

A Socratic seminar is a guided, yet free-flowing discussion about ideas that matter. They are lively conversations among teachers and students around the investigation of a great text, an inspiring work of art, or some other meaningful idea or concept worth discussing. To prepare for our Socratic seminar, let us examine some key pieces of information about this text by filling in the blank spaces of this *Socratic Seminar Prep Sheet*.

Author	
Title	
Literary Genre	
Date of Composition	

Key Ideas

The ideas we should understand well enough to analyze this particular text and evaluate the ideas within it.

Key Vocabulary

Words that are either so difficult, so crucial, or so abstract that they merit special consideration.

The "Big Idea"

This may be the central claim (or claims) that the author is trying to advance in his or her work, or it may be an idea that speaks to transcendent values such as truth, beauty, justice, and virtue. Or, the text may interact with deeply-rooted issues in the human condition so that no matter how long ago the text was written, it can speak to and inspire us today.

In short, the "Big Idea" is the most important idea or ideas circulating through this text.

Socratic Seminar / Conversation Map

A Socratic seminar is a guided, yet free-flowing discussion about ideas that matter. They are lively conversations among teachers and students around the investigation of a great text, an inspiring work of art, or some other meaningful idea or concept worth discussing. Use the space provided to take notes during the seminar.

In the space provided, consider drawing a conversation map, a visual representation of a seminar. To draw a conversation map, look around the room and take note of where each of your classmates is sitting; then write their initials on the space below in that order. As the seminar conversation moves forward, write down a brief comment about each contribution and a line connecting one speaker to another.

Works Cited

Adams, John. "Adams' Argument for the Defense: 3–4 December 1770." The National Archives: Founders Online, 18 Mar. 2018, https://founders.archives.gov/documents/Adams/05-03-02-0001-0004-0016. Accessed 20 Sept. 2022.

Adler, Mortimer J. and Charles Van Doren. *How to Read a Book: The Classic Guide to Intelligent Reading.* Simon & Schuster, 1972.

Aristotle. *Rhetoric.* Translated by W. Rhys. Roberts, MIT Classics Archive, 1924. http://classics.mit.edu/Aristotle/rhetoric.1.i.html

Bingham, Caleb, editor. *The Columbian Orator.* Forgotten Books, 2012.

Booth, Wayne C., Gregory G. Colomb, and Joseph M. Williams. *The Craft of Research.* University of Chicago Press, 2008.

Cicero. *Cicero on Oratory and Orators.* Translated by J. S. Watson, Alpha Editions, 2020.

Corbett, Edward P.J. *Classical Rhetoric for the Modern Student.* Oxford University Press, 1971.

Douglass, Frederick. *Frederick Douglass: Selected Speeches and Writings*, ed. Philip S. Foner (Chicago: Lawrence Hill, 1999), 188-206; "What to the Slave Is the Fourth of July?"" | Teaching American History." Teaching American History. Ashbrook Center at Ashland University, 2016. Web. 02 May 2016. <http://teachingamericanhistory.org/library/document/what-to-the-slave-is-the-fourth-of-july/>.

Henry, Patrick. "Liberty or Death." The Avalon Project, 2008, https://avalon.law.yale.edu/18th_century/patrick.asp. Accessed 20 Sept. 2022.

Humphreys, Justin. *"Aristotle."* Internet Encyclopedia of Philosophy, www.iep.utm.edu/aristotl/#H7.

Jackson, Andrew. "President Jackson's Veto Message Regarding the Bank of the United States; July 10, 1832." The Avalon Project, 2008, https://avalon.law.yale.edu/19th_century/ajveto01.asp. Accessed 20 Sept. 2022.

Jefferson, Thomas. "Thomas Jefferson to John Adams." Library of Congress, https://www.loc.gov/exhibits/jefferson/217.html#:~:text=I%20cannot%20live%20without%20books,is%20the%20only%20future%20object.

Kennedy, George Alexander. *Quintilian: A Roman Educator and His Quest for the Perfect Orator.* Sophron, 2017.

Kennedy, John F. "We Choose to Go to the Moon." John F. Kennedy Presidential Library and Museum, 18 Mar. 2018, <https://www.jfklibrary.org/asset-viewer/archives/JFKPOF/040/JFKPOF-040-001. Accessed 20 Sept. 2022>.

King Jr, Martin L. "I Have a Dream." Ashbrook Center at Ashland University, 2 May 2016, http://teachingamericanhistory.org/library/document/i-have-a-dream-speech/. Accessed 20 Sept. 2022.

Works Cited

Kraut, Richard. *"Plato."* Stanford Encyclopedia of Philosophy, Stanford University, 1 Aug. 2017, plato.stanford.edu/entries/plato/.

Kreeft, Peter. *Socratic Logic: A Logic Text Using Socratic Method, Platonic Questions, and Aristotelian Principles.* South Bend: St. Augustine Press, 2010.

Larsen, Aaron, and Joelle Hodge. *The Art of Argument: An Introduction to the Informal Fallacies.* Classical Academic Press, 2010.

Larsen, Aaron, et al. *The Discovery of Deduction: An Introduction to Formal Logic.* Classical Academic Press, 2009.

Lincoln, Abraham. "The Gettysburg Address." Abraham Lincoln Online, 2020, https://www.abrahamlincolnonline.org/lincoln/speeches/gettysburg.htm. Accessed 20 Sept. 2022.

Plato. *Plato on the Trial and Death of Socrates: Euthyphro, Apology, Crito, Phaedo.* Translated by Lane Cooper, Cornell University Press, 1977.

Quintilian. *Institutes of Oratory, or, Education of an Orator.* Edited by Curtis Dozier and Lee Honeycutt, translated by J. S. Watson, 2015.

Reagan, Ronald W. "A Time for Choosing." American Rhetoric, 2 Oct. 2021, https://www.americanrhetoric.com/speeches/ronaldreaganatimeforchoosing.htm. Accessed 20 Sept. 2022.

Shields, Christopher. *"Aristotle."* Stanford Encyclopedia of Philosophy. Stanford University, 25 Sept. 2008, plato.stanford.edu/entries/aristotle/

Turabian, Kate L. *A Manual for Writers of Research Papers, Theses, and Dissertations, Ninth Edition: Chicago Style for Students and Researchers.* University of Chicago Press, 2018.

Webster, Daniel. "Webster's Second Reply to Hayne." Teaching American History, n.d., https://teachingamericanhistory.org/document/the-webster-hayne-debates/. Accessed 20 Sept. 2022.

Zinsser, William. *On Writing Well: The Classic Guide to Writing Nonfiction.* Harper Collins, 2006.

Photography Credits

The photo of the United States Capitol Building in the Table of Contents is available via an Unsplash license, was made by user Harold Mendoza, and is accessible at <https://unsplash.com/photos/6xafY_AE1LM>.

Section I

The photo of Independence Hall is available via an Unsplash license, was made by user Tyler Rutherford, and is accessible at <https://unsplash.com/photos/Z4dYZKNiZ9Y>.

The photo of Independence Hall is available via an Unsplash license, was made by user Ernie Journeys, and is accessible at <https://unsplash.com/photos/M23cLuSb_Yo>.

The portrait of Quintilian is available in the public domain and may be found at <https://upload.wikimedia.org/wikipedia/commons/9/9a/Quintilian.jpg>.

The photo of the portrait of Demosthenes is available via a Creative Commons license, was made by userMarie-Lan Nguyen in 2011, and is accessible at <https://en.wikipedia.org/wiki/Demosthenes#/media/File:Demosthenes_Polyeuctos_Louvre_Ma237_n01.jpg>.

The portrait of Sir Winston Churchill is available in the public domain and is accessible at <https://en.wikipedia.org/wiki/Winston_Churchill#/media/File:Sir_Winston_Churchill_-_19086236948.jpg>.

The portrait of Dr. Martin Luther King, Jr. is available in the public domain and is accessible at <https://en.wikipedia.org/wiki/Martin_Luther_King_Jr.#/media/File:Martin_Luther_King,_Jr..jpg%3E>.

The painting of the Catiline Orations is available in the public domain and is accessible at <https://en.wikipedia.org/wiki/Catiline_Orations#/media/File:Maccari-Cicero.jpg>.

The Maryland State House is available via a Creative Commons license, was made by user Martin Falbisoner on September 6, 2013, and is accessible at <https://en.wikipedia.org/wiki/Maryland_State_House#/media/File:Maryland_State_House_from_College_Ave.JPG>.

The engraving of John Milton is available in the public domain and is accessible at <https://en.wikipedia.org/wiki/John_Milton#/media/File:John_Milton_1.jpg>.

The portrait of William Shakespeare is available in the public domain and is accessible at <https://en.wikipedia.org/wiki/William_Shakespeare#/media/File:Shakespeare.jpg>.

The portrait of Winston Churchill (cropped) is available in the public domain and is accessible at <https://en.wikipedia.org/wiki/Winston_Churchill#/media/File:Sir_Winston_Churchill_(cropped).jpg>.

The photograph of John F. Kennedy is available in the public domain and is accessible at <https://en.wikipedia.org/wiki/John_F._Kennedy#/media/File:John_F._Kennedy,_White_House_color_photo_portrait.jpg>.

The photo of the House of Burgesses is available in the public domain and is accessible at <https://en.wikipedia.org/wiki/House_of_Burgesses#/media/File:House_of_Burgesses_in_the_Capitol_Williamsburg_James_City_County_Virginia_by_Frances_Benjamin_Johnston.jpg>.

The photograph of the U.S. Senate chamber is available in the public domain and is accessible at <https://en.wikipedia.org/wiki/United_States_Capitol#/media/File:US_Senate_Chamber_c1873.jpg>.

The illustration by Walter Crane of Demosthenes leaving the Athenian Assembly in shame is available in the public domain and is accessible at <https://

Photography Credits

en.wikipedia.org/wiki/Demosthenes#/media/File:He_
lefts_assembly,_hiding_his_face_in_his_cloak.jpg>.

Section II

The photo of the U.S. Capitol Rotunda is available via
a Creative Commons license, was made by user Matt
H. Wade on September 9, 2005, and is accessible at
<https://en.wikipedia.org/wiki/United_States_Capitol#/
media/File:USCapitolRotunda.JPG>.

The photo of the interior of St. John's Episcopal Church
in Richmond is available in the public domain and
is accessible at < https://en.wikipedia.org/wiki/St._
John%27s_Episcopal_Church_(Richmond,_Virginia)#/
media/File:Detroit_Photographic_Company_(0841).jpg>.

The photo of the bust of Aristotle is available in
the public domain and may be accessed at <https://
en.wikipedia.org/wiki/Aristotle#/media/File:Aristotle_
Altemps_Inv8575.jpg>.

The photo of Ronald Reagan is available in the public
domain and is accessible at <https://commons.
wikimedia.org/wiki/File:Ronald_Reagan%27s_"A_Time_
for_Choosing"_speech_October_27,_1964.webm>.

The photo of the US Capitol, west side, is available via a
Creative Commons license, was made on September 5,
2013 by Martin Falbisoner, and is accessible at <https://
en.wikipedia.org/wiki/United_States_Capitol#/media/
File:US_Capitol_west_side.JPG>.

The painting depicting "Rhetoric" by Pieter Isaacsz
is available in the public domain and is accessible
at < https://en.wikipedia.org/wiki/Rhetoric#/media/
File:Knight_academy_lecture_(Rosenborg_Palace).jpg>.

The portrait of Frederick Douglass is available in the
public domain and is accessible at <https://upload.
wikimedia.org/wikipedia/commons/1/12/Unidentified_

Artist_-_Frederick_Douglass_-_Google_Art_Project-
restore.png>.

The photo of the US Capitol, east side, is available via a
Creative Commons license, was made on September 5,
2013 by Martin Falbisoner, and is accessible at <https://
en.wikipedia.org/wiki/United_States_Capitol#/media/
File:US_Capitol_west_side.JPG>.

Raphael's "School of Athens" is available in the public
domain and may be accessed at <https://en.wikipedia.
org/wiki/Aristotle#/media/File:Sanzio_01_Plato_
Aristotle.jpg>.

The illustration of Aristotle and Alexander the Great is
available in the public domain and may be accessed at
<https://commons.wikimedia.org/wiki/File:Alexander_
and_Aristotle.jpg>.

The photograph of the U.S. Senate chamber is available
in the public domain and is accessible at <https://
en.wikipedia.org/wiki/United_States_Capitol#/media/
File:US_Senate_Chamber_c1873.jpg>.

The photograph of the bust of Pericles is available
in the public domain and is accessible at <https://
commons.wikimedia.org/wiki/File:Pericles_Pio-
Clementino_Inv269_n2.jpg>.

The portrait of Abraham Lincoln is available in
the public domain and is accessible at <https://
en.wikipedia.org/wiki/Abraham_Lincoln#/media/
File:Abraham_Lincoln_O-77_matte_collodion_print.
jpg>.

The portrait of John Adams is available in the public
domain and is accessible at <https://en.wikipedia.org/
wiki/John_Adams#/media/File:Gilbert_Stuart,_John_
Adams,_c._1800-1815,_NGA_42933.jpg>.

Photography Credits

The portrait of Dr. Martin Luther King, Jr. is available in the public domain and is accessible at <https://en.wikipedia.org/wiki/Martin_Luther_King_Jr.#/media/File:Martin_Luther_King,_Jr..jpg%3E>.

The photo of the United States House of Representatives interior is available in the public domain and may be accessed at <https://en.wikipedia.org/wiki/United_States_House_of_Representatives#/media/File:United_States_House_of_Representatives_chamber.jpg>.

The illustration of Quintilian is from the frontispiece to a 1720 edition of *The Institutes of Oratory* available in the public domain and may be accessed at <https://en.wikipedia.org/wiki/Quintilian#/media/File:Quintilian,_Institutio_oratoria_ed._Burman_(Leiden_1720),_frontispiece.jpg>.

The photo of the statue of Socrates is available via Adobe Stock.

The painting, "The Death of Socrates" by Jacques-Louis David is available in the public domain and is accessible at <https://en.wikipedia.org/wiki/The_Death_of_Socrates#/media/File:David_-_The_Death_of_Socrates.jpg>.

The portrait of Patrick Henry is available in the public domain and is accessible at <https://en.wikipedia.org/wiki/Patrick_Henry#/media/File:Patrick_henry.JPG>.

The photograph of the bust of Cicero is available via a Creative Commons license, was made by user José Luiz Bernades Ribeiro on September 24, 2016, and is accessible at <https://en.wikipedia.org/wiki/Cicero#/media/File:Bust_of_Cicero_(1st-cent._BC)_-_Palazzo_Nuovo_-_Musei_Capitolini_-_Rome_2016.jpg>.

The portrait of Daniel Webster is available in the public domain and is accessible at <https://en.wikipedia.org/wiki/Daniel_Webster#/media/File:Daniel_Webster_Photograph_edited.jpg>.

The painting of "Webster's Reply to Hayne" by George P.A. Healy is available from the United States Senate and is accessible at <https://www.senate.gov/artandhistory/history/common/image/Websters_Reply_to_Hayne.htm>.

The photograph of the Governor's Mansion in Williamsburg, Virginia is available via an Unsplash license, was made by user Mateus Campos Felipe and is accessible at < https://unsplash.com/photos/qHPPP2rkLNE>.

The photo of the mountainside at the Oracle Delphi is available via a Creative Commons license, was made by user Helen Simonsson on May 11, 2012, and is accessible at <https://en.wikipedia.org/wiki/Socrates#/media/File:Delfi_Apollons_tempel.jpg>.

Glossary of Terms

A

A Statement: All S is P (*S* represents the subject; *P* represents the predicate).

Ad Baculum: The phrase *ad baculum* comes from the Latin phrase meaning "to the stick." This fallacy occurs whenever an individual tries to make someone fearful of the consequences of not siding with his or her argument.

Ad Hominem: An argument addressed "against the person" instead of dealing with the argument itself, from the Latin "to" or "against the man."

Ad Ignominiam: The phrase *ad ignominiam* comes from a Latin phrase meaning "to shame." This fallacy occurs whenever an individual tries to make someone else feel bad or shamed because of the position they hold in an argument.

Ad Misericordiam: The phrase *ad misericordiam* comes from Latin meaning "to pity." This fallacy occurs whenever someone makes an illegitimate appeal to pity in an argument, a debate, a paper, or in everyday conversation by making the audience feel sorry for someone or something.

Affirmative: When the proposition affirms something about the subject.

Alliteration: The repetition of a key consonants sounds in a sentence or a speech.

Anaphora: The repetition of key words or phrases from one sentence to another in order to reinforce the author's purpose.

Antecedent: In a hypothetical statement, this is the proposition that comes first after if. The word "antecedent" comes from the Latin "to go before," with the prefix "ante" meaning "before" or "in front of."

Argument: In logic, an argument is a group of statements containing reasons in support of a conclusion.

Aristotle: A Greek philosopher who lived from 384 to 322 BC; his writings, which include works such as *Politics, Poetics, Physics, Metaphysics,* and *Rhetoric*, form the basis for much of the Western canon.

Aristotle's Rules: These are the ways by which we can determine the validity of a syllogism. Some logic books cite six rules and others seven; our book cites seven rules.

Athens: A city in ancient Greece that, thanks to its wealth, its civic freedoms, and figures like Socrates, Plato, and Aristotle, was the birthplace of philosophy, democracy, and other components of the Western tradition.

Attentuata: A low or plain style of speaking, most appropriate for instructing.

C

Canon: The word canon comes from the Greek for measuring rod and refers to the standard or the criteria by which a piece of human culture is judged.

Categorical Form: The particular arrangement of terms in a proposition. A syllogism in categorical form contains three propositions each arranged in categorical form.

Categorical Logic: The kind of logic that focuses on the relationship between categories of things.

Categorical Propositions: A sentence written in categorical form and comprised of only the subject, predicate, copula, and quantifier.

Chiasmus: The careful balancing of clauses in a sentence, so that words and concepts are repeated and

Glossary of Terms

the same grammatical structure is used, but the words are arranged in a different order from one clause to the next.

Cicero: A Roman senator and statesman whom Quintilian believed came the closest to the *ideal orator*; a gifted orator, he was executed for denouncing the tyranny of Marc Anthony.

Complement: The complement opposite of a term. In logic we often form the complement by adding non- to the word since the complement represents everything the original term is not.

Compound Syllogism: A compound syllogism is a syllogism whose first premise is technically two different propositions; the second premise then affirms or denies a proposition in the first premise, leading to the conclusion.

Conclusion: The point to which an argument leads.

Confirmatio: As one of the *Six Parts of Discourse*, the speaker presents proof, evidence, and examples that support his overarching point.

Confutatio: As one of the *Six Parts of Discourse*, the speaker addresses the opposing arguments that may be raised against his speech.

Conjunctive Syllogism: A conjunctive syllogism is a compound syllogism that begins with a conjunctive statement, one using the correlating conjunctions *both* and *and*.

Conjuncts: The two clauses in a conjunctive syllogism, symbolized by the letters *P* and *Q*.

Consequent: In a hypothetical statement, this is the proposition that comes second (after *then*) . The word *consequent* comes from the Latin "to follow after," with the prefix "con" meaning "with."

Contradiction: The relationship between A and O statements, and between E and I statements. These pairs of statements cannot both be true at the same time; an A statement is proven false by an O statement (and vice-versa), and an E statement is proven false by an I statement (and vice-versa).

Contrariety: The relationship between A and E statements, in that two universal propositions with the same subject and the same predicate can both be false, but they cannot both be true.

Conversion: The process of interchanging the subject and predicate in a sentence to create an equivalent statement; conversion works on E statements, I statements, and partially on A statements.

Copula: A verb like *is* or *are* that refers to a state of being that the subject is in and helps connect the subject to its predicate.

Corollary: A proposition that is derived from a theorem that has already been given or has already been proven.

D

Declamation: Rhetorical exercises for students to practice composing and delivering speeches.

Deductive Reasoning: Reasoning that goes from specific premises to a general conclusion; deductive reasoning focuses more on the form and the structure of arguments. These arguments are often expressed in the form of a syllogism.

Deliberative Oratory: The kind of oratory used in any kind of assembly where some future course of action is debated.

Dependent Clause: A grammatical unit that contains both a subject and a verb but does not express a complete thought.

Glossary of Terms

Dialogue: A literary work where two or more speakers discuss a topic of philosophical significance.

Direct Inference: The act of drawing a conclusion from only one premise. Direct inference is also called immediate inference.

Disjunctive Syllogism: A compound syllogism built upon the correlating conjunction *either / or*; the wording of a disjunctive proposition implies that at least one of the propositions is true. If a logician denies either one of the two propositions, then its corresponding proposition must be true.

Dispositio: The arrangement or the outline of the material in your speech, paper, or other mode of communication.

Distribution: Distribution refers to how much of one term is identified with, or found in, the corresponding term it is joined to in a proposition. In negative propositions, *distribution* refers to the extent to which a term is excluded from its corresponding term.

Divisio: The speaker presents an outline of the points in his argument.

E

E Statement: No S is P (*S* represents the subject; *P* represents the predicate).

Elocutio: The canon of style and how polished and pleasing are the words in your speech.

Enthymeme: A syllogism with one premise omitted or "kept in mind"; these are especially important in rhetoric.

Equivocal Terms: Terms that can have more than one meaning or are ambiguous.

Ethos: This is not only your reputation but also how likable you are while you are speaking.

Exordium: The introduction to a speech.

Experience: The act of encountering the world and gathering information through the senses, such as our ability to see and hear.

F

Fallacy of an Affirmative Conclusion from a Negative Premise: This fallacy occurs when a syllogism has at least one negative premise and an affirmative conclusion.

Fallacy of a Negative Conclusion from Affirmative Premises: This fallacy occurs when a syllogism has a negative conclusion but has two affirmative premises.

Fallacy of Bifurcation: Also known as an *either / or* fallacy or a false dilemma, the fallacy of bifurcation falsely or illegitimately limits the number of options in an argument down to two, both of which are usually bad.

Fallacy of Equivocation: This fallacy occurs when the same term is used with two or more different meanings in the course of an argument.

Fallacy of Exclusive Premises: This fallacy occurs when a syllogism uses two negative premises.

Fallacy of Four Terms: This fallacy occurs when a syllogism has more than the three required terms.

Fallacy of Illicit Major: This fallacy occurs when major term is distributed in the conclusion but is not distributed in the major premise.

Fallacy of Illicit Minor: This fallacy occurs when the minor term is distributed in the conclusion but is not distributed in the minor premise.

Glossary of Terms

Fallacy of Illicit Process: This fallacy occurs when either the major or minor term is distributed in the conclusion but is not distributed in the premise in which that term first appears.

Fallacy of Moderation: The act of assuming the middle option or the compromise position is best based on the faulty assumption the middle ground is always best.

Fallacy of the False Cause: This fallacy occurs whenever we wrongly assume a *cause-and-effect* relationship exists between two events when, in reality, no real cause and effect relationship exists.

Fallacy of the Undistributed Middle: This fallacy occurs when the middle term is not distributed at least once in the syllogism.

Falsity: The notion that a proposition does not correspond to reality.

Figure: This idea refers to the location of the middle term in a syllogism.

First Order Enthymeme: An enthymeme where the implied proposition is the major premise.

First (1ˢᵗ) Figure: The middle term is the subject of the major premise and the predicate of the minor premise.

Five Canons of Rhetoric: The five most important components of a speech.

Florid: A flowery style, most appropriate for charming.

Formal Fallacy: A formal fallacy is an error in the structure of an argument so that its premises do not necessarily lead to its conclusion.

Formal Logic: Formal logic uses deductive reasoning and focuses on carefully structured arguments known as syllogisms.

Fourth (4ᵗʰ) Figure: The middle term is in the predicate of the major premise and the subject of the minor premise.

G

Grammar: The subject of grammar focuses on the rules of language and communication to read and understand texts and write in clear, intelligible prose; at times, grammar, as a road of the trivium, may also refer to the basic, fundamental building blocks of a subject.

Gravis: A heavy style, most appropriate for charming.

H

Hasty Generalization: A fallacy of inductive reasoning that occurs whenever we make a conclusion based on too few examples to justify this conclusion.

Hypothetical Syllogism: A hypothetical syllogism is a syllogism made up of two premises, the first premise being an if/then statement composed of two propositions; the second premise then affirms or denies one of the propositions in the first premise.

I

I Statement: Some S is P (*S* represents the subject; *P* represents the predicate).

Implication Sign: A symbol (⊃) for the hypothetical relationship between the antecedent. These symbols are used in hypothetical syllogisms.

Independent Clause: A grammatical unit that contains both a subject and a verb and also expresses a complete thought.

Inductive Reasoning: A form of reasoning that goes from observations to broad, universal principles.

Glossary of Terms

Inference: The third act of the mind, a process that takes information we do know and uses that information to reach a new conclusion.

Informal Fallacy: An informal fallacy is an error in the content of an argument.

Informal Logic: Informal logic includes more informal, ordinary language. Informal logic makes use of inductive reasoning and focuses more on the content of an argument as opposed to its structure.

Integrity: The ability and the willingness to do the right thing even if no one is looking.

Invalid: An argument is invalid if the conclusion does not follow logically from the premises; if the argument breaks any of the rules governing the formal construction of syllogisms.

Inventio: Not only the discovery, or invention, of the idea, but also the most effective means of arguing for that idea.

J

Judgment: The mental act of connecting one term with another to form a proposition.

Judicial (or Forensic) Oratory: The kind of oratory used in law courts, aimed at persuading a judge or a jury.

L

Liberal Arts: The liberal arts are composed of the *trivium* and the *quadrivium* and thus include grammar, logic, and rhetoric (the *trivium*) and music, arithmetic, geometry, and astronomy (*quadrivium*).

Logic: The art of right thinking and the ability to make sense of a wide array of facts and organize them into a coherent system.

Logician: An individual skilled in the art of right thinking, known as logic.

Logos: The appeal to reasoned argumentation.

M

Major Premise: The premise in which the major term (the predicate of the conclusion) originally appeared.

Major Term: The term used as the predicate in the conclusion of a syllogism.

Martin Luther King Jr.: In our own day, Martin Luther King Jr. comes close to that "ideal orator" for his commitment to justice and equality his incredible public speaking abilities.

Mediocre or Robusta: A middle or forcible style, most appropriate for moving or exhorting one's audience.

Memoria: The process of memorizing your speech.

Middle Term: The term appears in both premises and joins the major term and the minor term, but this term does not appear in the conclusion.

Minor Premise: The premise in which the minor term (the subject of the conclusion) originally appeared.

Minor Term: The term used as the subject in the conclusion of a syllogism.

Modus Ponens: The mode of *affirming the antecedent* or, translated from Latin "the mode that by affirming affirms." If the antecedent is true, then the consequent must also be true.

Modus Tollens: The mode of *denying the consequent* or, translated from Latin, "the mode that by denying denies." If we deny the consequent, then we can say with certainty that its corresponding antecedent is not true, either.

Glossary of Terms

Mood: The quality and quantity of the three propositions that comprise a syllogism.

N

Narratio: The speaker explains the nature of his case and why he is speaking.

Negative: When the proposition denies something about the subject.

O

O Statement: Some S is not P (*S* represents the subject; *P* represents the predicate).

Obversion: The process of negating the predicate of a proposition and changing the quality of that statement to create an equivalent statement. These work for all statement types.

Oracle at Delphi: The Greek world had a number of oracles who gave pronouncements about the future; the Oracle at Delphi was among the most famous.

P

Panegyric Oratory: The kind of oratory used at solemn state occasions.

Parallelism: The use of grammatically-balanced words, phrases, or clauses in a speech which not only sound better but also convey a sense of balance and order.

Partial Conversion: Because the subject and predicate terms in an A statement are not evenly distributed, an A statement can only be partially-converted. After interchanging the subject and the predicate, A statements must be changed to I statements.

Particular: The notion that a proposition only discusses or touches upon one particular, undefined group within the subject.

Pathos: The appeal to the emotions.

Peroratio: The conclusion of a speech.

Plato: A student of Socrates and Athenian philosopher; his writings serve as the basis for much of Western philosophy. He lived from around 428 to 347 BC.

Polysyndeton: The excessive use of conjunctions in a sentence in order to convey a sense of excitement and urgency.

Post Hoc Ergo Propter Hoc: Latin for "after this; therefore because of this," this fallacy assumes that because one event happened after another, that the first event caused the other; however, this need not be the case.

Predicate: The part of the sentence that describes or renames the subject.

Premise: The reasons given in an argument that lead to its conclusion.

Pronuntiatio: The process of delivering your speech.

Proposition: A sentence that joins together a term with another term in order to communicate some idea about the world, an idea that could either be true or false.

Q

Quadrivium: The place where the "four roads meet," with those four roads being music, arithmetic, geometry, and astronomy.

Quality: The notion that a proposition may affirm or deny something about the subject.

Quantifiers: These are words such as *all*, *some*, *some... not* or *no* and indicate the quantity and the quality of a given proposition.

Quantity: The notion that a subject is either universal or particular.

Glossary of Terms

Quintilian: A Roman educator who believed that the ideal orator should not only be an eloquent speaker, but also a lover of wisdom and virtue.

R

Reason: The ability to solve complicated problems, think about subjects of great difficulty, and contemplate issues over and above everyday human experience.

Reductio ad absurdam: A form of *modus tollens* that begins by assuming the consequent is true, then draws out a series of ridiculous conclusions that follow after, all of which show that the consequent can, in fact, not be true.

Relationships of Equivalence: These are ways to alter a proposition to create ones that have the same meaning.

Rhetoric: The art of public speaking, which the ancient world considered an important component of public service.

Rhetorical Devices: An arrangement of words in such a way that these words sound more pleasing, carry more meaning, and thus should be more memorable.

S

Schema: A means of identifying a syllogism by its mood and its figure.

Scholastics: A group of medieval scholars and professors who gave names to syllogisms to help them determine whether or not those syllogisms were valid.

Second (2nd) Figure: The middle term is in the predicate of both the major premise and the minor premise.

Second Order Enthymeme: An enthymeme where the implied proposition is the minor premise.

Simple Apprehension: This is the first act of the mind that focuses on the clear understanding of terms.

Simple Sentence: A sentence with only one subject and one predicate.

Six Parts of Discourse: The division of a speech into different parts including the introduction, the statement of the case, answers to opposing arguments, and the conclusion of the speech.

Slippery Slope: The *slippery slope* fallacy occurs whenever we assume that one event will necessarily cause a sequence of other events, especially if that event and subsequent events are undesirable and negative.

Socrates: A Greek philosopher and "gadfly of Athens" whose incessant questioning and probing into the nature of the good life led to his execution in 399 BC. He lived from 470 to 399 BC.

Sophists: A group of teachers of rhetoric who taught wealthy Athenians how to speak well in public. They did not have much, if any, regard for the truth.

Sound: If an argument employs valid reasoning and all of the propositions are true, then that argument is sound.

Square of Opposition: As formulated by Aristotle, this is a visual way of showing the relationships between categorical propositions, providing that they all have the same subject and predicate terms.

Straw Man Fallacy: This fallacy occurs when we take our opponent's argument and make it appear as weak, as stupid, or as ridiculous a version of our opponent's real argument as possible. Then, we go and refute that idea instead of their real argument.

Glossary of Terms

Subalternate Moods: These are syllogism forms that were not included in the original list of mnemonic devices, but they are valid under the rule of subalterns.

Subalternation: The relationship between A statements and I statements and between E statements and O statements, in that the truth of the universal proposition (A, E statements) implies the truth of the particular proposition (I, O statements) with the same subject and predicate. The relationship between I statements and A statements, and between O statements and E statements, in that if a particular statement (I, O statements) is false, then by necessity, its corresponding universal proposition (A, E statements) must be false, too.

Subcontrariety: The relationship between I and O statements, in that two particular propositions with the same subject and the same predicate can both be true, but they cannot both be false.

Subject: The main actor in a sentence; what the sentence is about.

Sweeping Generalization: A fallacy of inductive reasoning that occurs when we take a general rule and apply it to a more narrowed, focused, specific situation or to examples where that generalization does not apply.

Syllogism: A formal, structured argument composed of two premises leading to a conclusion; the written expression of the mental act of inference.

T

Term: This is the simplest, most fundamental unit of meaning. A term is the written expression of concept that is "held" or "apprehended" in the mind when we think of a particular idea or concept.

Third Order Enthymeme: An enthymeme where the implied proposition is the conclusion.

Three Acts of the Mind: The three steps that human beings can progress through when thinking, which are the acts of simple apprehension, judgment, and inference.

Three Modes of Persuasion: The Greek philosopher Aristotle identified three different ways or modes of persuasion; they include *ethos*, *logos*, and *pathos*.

Third (3ʳᵈ) Figure: The middle term is the subject of both the major and the minor premise.

Tilda: A symbol (~) used when we say that an idea (such as P or Q) is false.

Trivium: A three-fold approach to education that began with grammar, continued with logic, and ended with rhetoric; the metaphorical place where the "three roads" of grammar, logic, and rhetoric meet.

Truth: The notion that a proposition corresponds to reality.

Tu Quoque Fallacy: From the Latin "you also," this is the act of responding to your opponents' criticism by criticizing your opponent's experience on that same matter.

U

Unconvertible Statements: Because the subject and predicate terms in an O statement are not evenly distributed, an O statement does not convert at all.

Universal: The notion that the proposition discusses or encompasses the entire category of the subject.

Glossary of Terms

V

Valid: An argument in which the conclusion follows logically from the premises; the argument follows all the rules governing the construction of syllogisms.

Venn Diagram: A visual way of testing syllogisms for validity that uses three overlapping circles to show the relationship between terms.

Virtue: The habits of moral excellence that often include character traits like honesty, integrity, hard work, and courage.

Z

Zeugma: A verb or an adjective that is used in two different ways and thus joins together two different parts of a sentence.

NEVER ✦ CEASE
LEARNING

© 2023 THALES PRESS

Made in the USA
Columbia, SC
11 February 2025

53540382R00096